LETTING
DATA
LEAD

How to **Design, Analyze,** and **Respond** to **Classroom Assessment**

EILEEN DEPKA

the **Solution Tree**
Assessment Center

555 North Morton Street
Bloomington, IN 47404
800.733.6786 (toll free) / 812.336.7700
FAX: 812.336.7790

email: info@SolutionTree.com
SolutionTree.com

Visit **go.SolutionTree.com/assessment** to download the free reproducibles in this book.

Printed in the United States of America

Library of Congress Cataloging-in-Publication Data

Names: Depka, Eileen, author.
Title: Letting data lead : how to design, analyze, and respond to classroom
    assessment / Eileen Depka.
Description: Bloomington, IN : Solution Tree Press, [2019] | Includes
    bibliographical references and index.
Identifiers: LCCN 2018040014 | ISBN 9781947604193 (perfect bound)
Subjects: LCSH: Educational tests and measurements. | Educational evaluation.
    | Education--Data processing. | Academic achievement.
Classification: LCC LB3051 .D444 2019 | DDC 370.285--dc23 LC record available at
    https://lccn.loc.gov/2018040014

Solution Tree
Jeffrey C. Jones, CEO
Edmund M. Ackerman, President

Solution Tree Press
President and Publisher: Douglas M. Rife
Associate Publisher: Sarah Payne-Mills
Art Director: Rian Anderson
Managing Production Editor: Kendra Slayton
Senior Editor: Amy Rubenstein
Proofreader: Elisabeth Abrams
Text Designer: Jill Resh
Cover Designer: Laura Cox
Editorial Assistant: Sarah Ludwig

ACKNOWLEDGMENTS

I'd like to extend a huge thank-you to all of the wonderful folks at Solution Tree for their dedication to the development of resources that support and grow the expertise of all educators. A special thanks to Douglas Rife for his continued support and kindness, and to Sarah Payne-Mills for her flexibility, leadership, and guidance.

Solution Tree Press would like to thank the following reviewers:

Jamie Lakey
Assistant Principal
Coppell Middle School North
Coppell, Texas

Jesse Morrill
Principal
Kinard Middle School
Fort Collins, Colorado

Kristin Poage
Assistant Principal
Jackson Creek Middle School
Bloomington, Indiana

Jim Wysocki
Math Teacher
Catlin Gabel School
Portland, Oregon

Visit **go.SolutionTree.com/assessment** to download the free reproducibles in this book.

TABLE OF CONTENTS

ABOUT THE AUTHOR

 **Eileen Depka, PhD,** has a background in assessment, common assessment design, rubric development, standards-based assessment, question design, classroom questioning practices, positive practices in grading and reporting, and the implementation of standards-based grading and reporting. She is the author of many books including *Bringing Homework Into Focus, Using Formative Assessment in the RTI Framework, Designing Rubrics for Mathematics, Designing Assessment for Mathematics,* and *The Data Guidebook for Teachers and Leaders.*

Eileen has supervised and coordinated curriculum, instruction, assessment, special education, educational technology, and continuous improvement efforts. She has taught all subjects at the elementary and middle school levels as well as graduate-level courses. She provides professional development for K–12 and undergraduate educators and, as a consultant, has worked across the country, focusing on creating engaging workshops tailored to meet a school's and district's individual needs.

She is passionate about student achievement and believes that all students can find academic success. Her goal is to work with teachers and administrators to collectively increase expertise and add to strategy banks used in schools to increase student performance.

Eileen earned a bachelor's degree in elementary and middle level education from the University of Wisconsin–Milwaukee, and she earned her master's and doctorate degrees from Cardinal Stritch University.

To learn more about Eileen's work, follow @eileen_depka on Twitter.

To book Eileen Depka for professional development, contact pd@SolutionTree .com.

INTRODUCTION

Wouldn't it be incredible if the word *data* was always synonymous with *action*? Now that we have the data, *what* do we do? *How* do we respond after we have assessed students? *What* type of data do we collect, and *how* do we know what to do after we collect it? The intention of this book is to look at data from classroom assessment, whether formative or summative, whether common or administered in a single classroom. With classroom assessment in mind, the pages that follow highlight practices through a cycle of assessment that will clarify responses prior to administering the assessment and throughout developing and administering any assessment.

It is through our preplanning and forethought prior to giving an assessment that data become actionable. Although data provide insights into which students or concepts need attention, preplanning gives us a road map into the very important next steps. When developing assessments, we start at the very beginning of a unit of study and identify the standards, content, and level of proficiency. This is the first time we consider the response to data. Assessments allow students multiple opportunities to demonstrate proficiency, and with each assessment, teachers consider in advance how to respond to the results. Next, during lesson development, teachers consider the reteaching process. This approach is time efficient and prepares, in advance, a plan of how and when to respond should students experience difficulty. It's also important to consider the time to respond and how to give students an integral role in planning and implementing the response. The goal is that, when educators analyze data, they have previously defined actions capable of boosting student understanding that can be immediately implemented.

This book provides systems, processes, and examples that offer an insight into this cycle of assessment.

About This Book

The following overview provides a brief insight into the areas of concentration within each chapter.

Chapter 1: Designing Assessments—Where Data Response Starts

Chapter 1 provides and defines the process of assessment. The use of a cyclical approach to assessment assists in connecting how a data response is considered at the early stages of assessment development and clearly defined prior to assessment implementation. It sets the stage for the ideas shared throughout the chapters.

The chapter continues to make a connection between assessment design and meaningful data. The chapter distinguishes between mistakes and misunderstandings to best determine whether the data designate the need for a response and which type of response is most appropriate. Examples set the stage for responding to data during the assessment development process by aligning questions to standards as well as determining a potential response if students are unable to proficiently respond to the questions. Teachers will gain strategies to align their expected response with students' response to data.

Chapter 2: Creating a Structure to Support Data Consistency for Common Assessments

The common assessment design process is at the center of attention in chapter 2; however, the content relates to single classroom assessment implementation as well. In other words, although the chapter highlights the work of teams, individual teachers can also use the approach in a single classroom. The methods the chapter suggests apply to any type of assessment, whether a quick check of student progress or those categorized as formative or summative. The purpose is not how a team, or a teacher, designs the assessment but the implementation process. Also discussed is the need to identify proficiency whether the assessment is common or used in a single classroom. Knowing in advance how students need to perform in order to show they understand is necessary to effectively evaluate the data. The chapter also considers the number of test items and how many times a student needs to demonstrate a performance accurately and acceptably in order to be considered proficient.

Chapter 3: Visualizing and Interpreting Data With an Eye on Action

Chapter 3 includes recommendations, examples, and rubrics that exemplify a connection between the assessment, visualization and interpretation of data, and consideration of the response. Academic data are a focus, yet the chapter also highlights perceptions and attitudinal data as important sources of student information.

Chapter 4: Responding to Data—Considerations, Practices, and Procedures

Chapter 4 makes a distinction between a *mistake* and a *misunderstanding*. Students can self-correct a mistake. However, a misunderstanding creates the need for additional learning. A systematic approach to lesson design, implementation, and response is explained. The approach identifies responding to data as a proactive design option. Because the team or teachers identify the response during lesson design, it is automatic and implemented immediately after they've analyzed results. Suggestions offer ways to find time to respond to misunderstandings.

Chapter 5: Encouraging Students to Respond to Data

Providing students the opportunity to evaluate and understand their learning needs supports their ability to learn and grow. Chapter 5 concentrates on methods to involve students in analysis of their personal data. It stresses the importance of engaging students in processes and systems that cause them to evaluate their strengths and challenges, track their data, and set goals to improve performance.

Chapter 6: Considering Sustainability

Chapter 6 suggests considerations that do not involve assessment, data, or response but can impact the success of a process that supports efforts to achieve positive results with students. The chapter is intended to provide information for teachers, teacher leaders, and school leaders. It also serves as a brief summary of key process points expressed throughout previous chapters.

The Goal

Letting Data Lead emphasizes the goal: prior to ever collecting and reviewing data, teams and teachers identify an action plan to implement as soon as data are available. This book's contents encourage and support the design, analysis, and response to classroom assessment through proactive planning. In the following chapters, you'll discover how to truly let data lead.

CHAPTER 1

Designing Assessments: Where Data Response Starts

Teaching is no easy task. The drive, passion, and motivation that bring teachers into the profession are far beyond a cursory knowledge or love of a topic. It, instead, demands that we have the ability to respond to the ever-increasing needs of students and the drive to continue learning. Having the capacity to continue to learn and grow can be difficult, yet the profession is rewarding. Directly related to our capability to impact the lives of our students is the regular use of assessment data. James Popham (2008), an educational author, says, "Effective testing will enhance a teacher's instructional effectiveness" (p. 1). It will also support the ability to respond to data both accurately and appropriately.

Data alone can take us only to a point, but no further. They provide evidence of performance, yet that is not the intended end; it is just a start. The goal is to relate the data to educational improvement. Through carefully considering and identifying the purpose, data become information, and information leads us to action (Campbell & Levin, 2008).

It's probably not unusual to think that the way we respond to data starts after the data are collected and analyzed. However, if we consider a shift in order, the response could be automatic. In this chapter, we will consider that shift. Process can support the ability to respond to data through preplanning. Let's go to the very beginning to better understand the end. Dylan Wiliam (2011), in his book *Embedded Formative Assessment*, states, "When the focus is on the decision that needs to be made, the teacher can then look at relevant sources of evidence that would contribute to making that decision in a smarter way" (p. 45). The pages that follow suggest decisions about the response to data. *How* will we respond to data? *When* do we respond, and *when* do we move on? *What* actions will we take in an effort to respond to data? Teachers and teams consider and identify the answers to these questions during lesson development so that once the data are available, the action is already clearly defined.

In this chapter, we discuss assessment design, starting with detailing the system of assessment crucial to the assessment process. We look specifically at identifying the learning that is essential to student understanding and the importance of aligning questions to standards. The chapter goes on to link the student response to questions teachers ask to the expected response in order to evaluate student understanding or address the lack of understanding. Finally, the chapter connects the assessment, the data analysis, and the response to indicate that preplanning the response links the assessment to data and clearly identifies next steps.

Understanding the System of Assessment

Consider responding to data as a crucial step in an assessment cycle. With student achievement as the goal, we create a routine in which data are essential. The approach to assessment is systematic, the purpose of which is to guide and direct instructional decisions in order to meet the needs of all students (Hamilton et al., 2009). That being said, the focus needs to be on the response to student needs, and although data are the source of information, it is the action that will promote enhanced student achievement. That action, if identified during the unit design process, can be immediate. Let's consider that process.

During the unit design process, we start with identifying standards, proceed to determining the unit targets, create the tools to use for assessment, and design lessons to enable students to reach the desired outcomes. Teams and teachers identify strategies to use and the methods to employ during lesson design and tweak and adjust them throughout implementation to meet students' needs. It is during the unit design process that we begin to identify the responses needed should individuals or groups of students require additional support (see figure 1.1). Figure 1.1 illustrates this system of assessment. It's important to note that the steps are continuous and repeated over time; they do not just occur once. Although teachers may implement the response to data at the end of the system of assessment, that response involves careful planning throughout the assessment process to ensure students do not fall behind.

When preparing to implement a unit, identifying standards and outcomes is step one. Knowing what we are going to teach provides the targets needed so that we can create a road map of assessments, lessons, and strategies that enable students to reach the target. This identification process not only assists in unit design but is essential for evaluating practices and strategies to best teach the lessons.

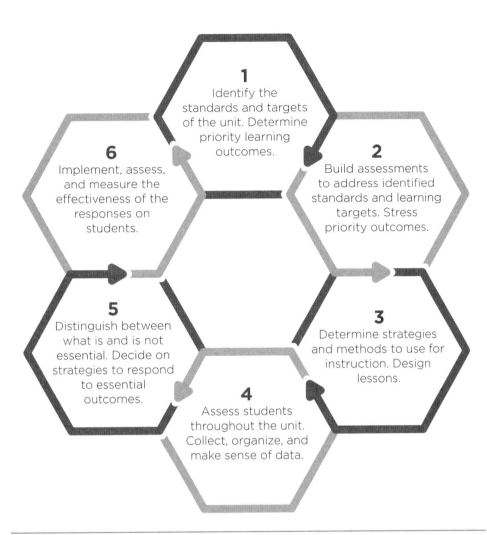

1
Identify the standards and targets of the unit. Determine priority learning outcomes.

2
Build assessments to address identified standards and learning targets. Stress priority outcomes.

3
Determine strategies and methods to use for instruction. Design lessons.

4
Assess students throughout the unit. Collect, organize, and make sense of data.

5
Distinguish between what is and is not essential. Decide on strategies to respond to essential outcomes.

6
Implement, assess, and measure the effectiveness of the responses on students.

Figure 1.1: System of assessment.

Step two recommends that time be spent building assessments. Starting with a summative assessment ensures that the expected unit outcomes are included in a summative piece. The assessment illustrates that which we expect students to know, do, and apply as the result of new learning. Formative assessments should be incorporated throughout the lesson in an effort to regularly provide practice opportunities and monitor the progress of students as they connect with new outcomes, content, or standards. If students are having difficulty, the consistent use of formative practices will help identify confusion and weakness before they become difficult to overcome. To clarify, *summative* doesn't mean only at the end of a chapter or unit, but any time students have had ample opportunity to practice new concepts and should be able to demonstrate proficiency according to the time and opportunities they have had with the concepts being assessed. If students are experiencing success with their practice opportunities, it would be an appropriate time for a summative assessment. Teachers often employ formative assessments daily to practice new content and quickly evaluate class progress, such as with exit tickets or other methods.

As teachers design assessments or identify them in existing resources, time should be spent ensuring that the questions and tasks clearly align with the identified targets. The alignment should also be connected to the strategies to teach students the concepts and relate to how students practiced and applied the skills. This alignment is useful when evaluating the strategies and techniques that worked in teaching the unit and those that did not have an outcome acceptable to us. During reteaching, we make use of the strategies and practices that had a previous productive impact on student results. Teaching concepts in the same way they were taught originally could result in a continued lack of understanding if the desired success was not achieved. Therefore, having alternative strategies identified will assist students in achieving proficiency at an acceptable level.

The third step in this process is to pinpoint strategies and create lessons that will engage students in learning activities to help them understand the identified content. Consider how the lessons will be introduced. Determine if direct instruction is needed. Examine the methods to engage students in the learning process. Will there be large- and small-group discussions? What independent assignments will students engage in? How will technology support learning with the identified content and lessons? Will content be differentiated in any way? What types of questions will students be asked to support academic success and encourage rigor?

Step four includes incorporating formative and summative assessments along the way. This provides the opportunity to evaluate and respond to student progress in an ongoing approach. Student assessment includes any and all activities in which students are asked to demonstrate understanding. This could include brief assignments, projects, discussions, performances, conversations, and any other methods deemed appropriate for students to demonstrate the knowledge, skills, and applications important to their success in reaching the intended unit outcomes. Assessments are considered formative as students first become acquainted with the topics. Summative assignments, often associated with grading, can be frequent and assigned as students have had the time and practice deemed necessary in order to be successful.

When students engage in activities to demonstrate their abilities and levels of understanding, there is an expectation that they'll receive a response indicating how they performed compared to the expectation. The review of that work, both for individual students and collectively for the class, results in feedback and actions that propel students to higher levels of success. The more immediate the response, the greater the possibility of a quicker rate of accomplishment. Feedback promotes understanding and growth. In order to best understand next steps, students can be encouraged to use the feedback, evaluate their current status, and determine the steps they will take and the support they will need in order to move forward.

Step five indicates that our response to student misunderstanding includes identifying the learning that is essential. Time and effort are best placed with the skills and concepts that impact future lessons and have endurance over time. Identify what students need to know and apply for continued success. For those concepts and procedures, a response is required. Any targets that will be repeated throughout the year, and are not essential for the moment, may result in a conversation and be important to monitor in the future. Those concepts likely do not require an immediate and detailed response. Time is precious and limited, so identifying the essential will make the best use of that which is available.

After determining the essential, a plan is identified to respond to aspects of the assessment that require immediate attention. At this point, we refer back to how the targets were taught during the unit. What instruction is required? Does the teacher need to teach the concepts using an alternative method to result in greater understanding? What responsibilities lie with the students in deepening their understanding? What will students need to do in order to demonstrate that they have acquired the knowledge and skills? The response is then implemented and monitored to evaluate student success.

High-quality assessment data can and will improve instruction and impact student results. An understanding of how to review and interpret data supports data analysis (Protheroe, 2009). When considering what we do with the information acquired through data analysis, the scope of the possibilities is not limited to reteaching. It could include changing a strategy, providing a tool, celebrating, allowing additional time, and so on. We analyze misconceptions and determine if students understood the expectations. At that point, we determine what, if any, action is necessary.

Identifying the Essential Standards

At each grade level or in each course, dozens of standards are present. Prioritizing the assessment contents will assist in determining when a data response is necessary and when additional time and continued learning will be the only response needed. Think about the assessment from the perspective of nice to know and necessary to know. The "nice to knows" might provide background knowledge.

It could be facts that can be researched when needed, or might be enhancements or peripheral information that surrounds or supports the topic but isn't essential to future understanding. The "necessary to knows" include all that is essential to demonstrate an understanding of the topic and apply the knowledge and skills crucial to future success. If something is necessary to know, a response to misconceptions is required. As alluded to earlier, the timing of the response depends upon when students need the knowledge and skills for future success. If there are additional opportunities and the ability to demonstrate understanding is spread throughout the year, responding to the data can take place over time.

Let's talk about the difference between nice to know and necessary to know. As an example, a nice to know in mathematics is the basic facts. You might even consider them extremely helpful in the ease at which a student is able to engage in mathematics as time goes on. However, if a student is having great difficulty with memorization, tools are available to assist him or her. Understanding the thought processes to solve real-world problems is a high priority. If memorization becomes a losing battle for students, successful use of procedures, logical thinking, and problem-solving techniques and engaging in complex tasks can still be possible for them.

In science, although I might like students to know the parts of a plant, the essential likely lies in the functions of those parts, what plants need to survive, and how environment changes the looks and needs of a plant. I am not trying to make light of encouraging students to commit crucial information to memory; however, the reason we have students commit something to memory is so they can access it more easily to understand deeper and more complex concepts quickly. We don't want a student's inability to memorize to limit his or her access to deeper, richer content.

In order to best understand when a response to lack of understanding is immediately needed, consider the questions that follow when both designing and evaluating an assessment.

- What portions of the assessment require immediate understanding to move to the next level of learning? An immediate response is required.

- What concepts in this assessment are important to student success in other subjects? An immediate response is required.

- What portions of the assessment will not be taught again and are important to long-term student success? An immediate response is required.

- What portions of the assessment will be taught and re-evaluated throughout the year? An awareness of continued progress is required.

- Does the student demonstrate understanding of the same concept on other portions of the assessment? In other words, is the error a simple mistake or a misunderstanding? Misunderstandings should be clarified. The student can correct a mistake.

- Is the incorrect response more factual in nature? If it can be researched, the student can be asked to do so and correct the response.

Aligning Questions to Standards and Data Response

In an effort to identify what students are to know, do, and apply in each grade or course, we look to state standards. Through the guidance of the standards document, the learning outcomes are determined. Careful consideration during this part of the planning process assists in the data analysis and action phase following assessment administration.

As an example, we can look at a writing standard. If the standard is dissected into its parts, that which the student needs to know and do becomes clear. Figure 1.2 (page 12) provides an example of one method that can be used when determining the specific expectations defined within the standard. This definition leads to an understanding by the teacher and students as to what the expectations are.

Part one of figure 1.2 lists all sections of the second Common Core writing standard for grade five. The second part of the template lists specific actions students should meet in order to achieve the standard. The verbs listed in the first column indicate the actions that students must engage in. They also provide direction for assessment and lesson design. The verbs indicate what actions the students will engage in when demonstrating proficiency. The second column indicates the specifics listed in the standard providing detail regarding what is receiving the action. For example, in this standard, the students are introducing a topic, providing focus, grouping related information, and so on. The first and second columns show a condensed and easy-to-review version of all that appears in the standard. The third column provides any specific information or details that highlight further actions necessary to achieve the standard. In many cases, the third column is blank because the standard does not include additional information.

W.5.2: Write informative/explanatory texts to examine a topic and convey ideas and information clearly.

    a. Introduce a topic clearly, provide a general observation and focus, and group related information logically; include formatting (e.g., headings), illustrations, and multimedia when useful to aiding comprehension.

    b. Develop the topic with facts, definitions, concrete details, quotations, or other information and examples related to the topic.

    c. Link ideas within and across categories of information using words, phrases, and clauses (e.g., in *contrast*, *especially*).

    d. Use precise language and domain-specific vocabulary to inform about or explain the topic.

    e. Provide a concluding statement or section related to the information or explanation presented.

Dissecting the Standard

What action is the student being asked to do?	What receives the action?	Why or how will students illustrate the action (if stated in the standard)?
Introduce	• Topic	
Provide	• Observation • Focus	
Group	• Related information	
Include	• Formatting • Illustrations • Multimedia	• To aid comprehension
Develop	• Topic	• With facts • With definitions • With details • With quotations • Using other information • Using other examples
Link	• Ideas	• Using words • Using phrases • Using clauses
Use	• Precise language • Domain-specific vocabulary	
Provide	• Concluding statement	

Source for standard: National Governors Association Center for Best Practices (NGA) & Council of Chief State School Officers (CCSSO), 2010a.

Figure 1.2: Dissecting the standard from an assessment perspective.

In order to illustrate the connection between the standard and the assessment, let's focus on the first criterion listed in figure 1.2 which is the introduction of the topic. The goal of any assessment is to enable students to show, in multiple ways, that they understand and can apply the knowledge and skills desired to meet expectations. The goal of the assessment is not only to make sure that students can fulfill the task. It is also necessary to have the assessment help indicate where difficulties lie if students are unsuccessful at the task. As a result, the brief assessment in figure 1.3 (page 14) is an example that provides detail helpful to data analysis and action. It provides students the opportunity to not only write a topic introduction, but to analyze the components of a quality introduction. As a result, if students have difficulty with their writing, the other tasks in the assessment help us to understand why they struggled. Do they have the knowledge and skills necessary to complete what is asked of them? If they don't, the assessment should be designed in such a way that any difficulty students are having is apparent somewhere within the assessment.

To clarify, let's take a look at figure 1.3. Parts one through three include foundational skills that support student ability to complete the task. The students are providing their insights, which contribute to our body of evidence indicating whether they are recognizing the level of quality required to apply their knowledge and skills by writing a quality introduction. Part four provides the opportunity to create an actual introduction. If they are able to select a topic of choice, students are empowered and may feel more secure in their ability to write about the topic chosen.

This assessment is focused on a single topic, which narrows the scope of a response to data should one be deemed necessary. It is structured in a way to pinpoint and evaluate student strengths and challenge areas throughout the assessment during the design process. Students engage in specific questions that are scaffolded so that they demonstrate understanding prior to entering the next level of complexity. The goal is to identify weaknesses as soon as possible so any misunderstandings can be clarified and skills can be bolstered. When there is assurance that students have the foundation necessary to be successful writing the introduction, the preliminary questions are no longer necessary. Students are ready to engage in the process, and the assessment can be designed without the initial questions.

The scaffolded questions are necessary in the beginning because if we go to advanced questions immediately and students aren't successful, it is difficult to determine why. What did they not understand? The foundational questions assist in helping us to best understand why and where mistakes occur.

Part 1: Choose the best opening sentence for the topic listed. Explain why you feel that is the best opening.

Topic 1—Baseball

    A. I'm going to tell you all about baseball.

    B. Baseball is a sport where you use a ball and a bat.

    C. Two teams, nine innings, and lots of excitement—that's baseball!

The best opening sentence is letter _____.

I think that is the case because

Part 2: Below each topic sentence, share your opinion about the quality of the sentence and how it could be improved.

Topic 2—The Camel

    A. In order to best understand the camel, it is important to know where it lives, what it eats, and why it is important to humans.

    B. I'm going to tell you all about camels.

    C. Camels are interesting and unusual animals.

Part 3: What advice would you give to someone who needs to create a well-written topic introduction?

Part 4: Choose one of the topics below and write an introduction to the topic. Include only the points you feel are important to the introduction.

- My Family
- Getting to Know ME!
- All About My School

Figure 1.3: Sample assessment—introducing a topic.

Part four of figure 1.3 can be evaluated with a standards-based rubric which provides the criteria important to student success taken directly from the standards (see figure 1.4). Quality indicators are also presented at each point value for each criterion. A benefit of using the rubric is that it provides feedback

W.5.2a: Introduce a topic clearly, provide a general observation and focus.				
	1	2	3	4
Clarity	Topic is not addressed.	Topic is confusing.	Topic is clearly stated.	Topic is clearly stated with supportive details.
General Observation	Topic is not addressed.	Topic is addressed.	Topic is addressed and forecasts content of piece.	Topic is addressed and forecasts content of piece with supportive detail.
Focus	Introduction is scattered with no understandable focus.	Introduction has focus.	Introduction is focused and relates to topic.	Introduction is focused, relates to topic, and sets the stage for the rest of the piece.

Source for standard: NGA & CCSSO, 2010a.

Figure 1.4: Sample rubric—evaluation of topic introductions.

to students about their performance. They can see the descriptors assigned to their performance as well as those indicating what it takes to achieve the next level of success.

No matter the subject, topic, or standards associated with the assessment, design should include the foundational skills that lead to tasks and applications designed within the assessments. This is necessary with assessments so that the data can be analyzed and an effective response identified. Sometimes in an effort to gain rigor, it is possible that we eliminate that which we feel students should already know. If the skills are foundational to the next level of success, design questions to include even the "easy" until we are certain that students have the foundational skills, and the questions are no longer needed to understand why errors may occur.

Figure 1.5 (page 16) provides a mathematics example of aligning assessment questions to a specific standard. This assessment is designed to evaluate student understanding of terminology associated with the mathematics as well as the standard itself. The goal is to have students demonstrate their understanding of parallel and perpendicular lines as well as right angles. Students should be able to use their knowledge to categorize shapes.

4.G.A.2: Classify two-dimensional figures based on the presence or absence of parallel or perpendicular lines, or the presence or absence of angles of a specified size. **Recognize** right triangles as a category, and identify right triangles.

1. Using the space provided and an appropriate tool, draw a set of parallel lines.

2. Using the space provided and an appropriate tool, draw a set of perpendicular lines.

3. Using the space provided and an appropriate tool, draw a right angle.

Label each shape using all of the following words that apply: *parallel, perpendicular, right angle.* If none apply, write the word *none.*

4. □   5. ⏢   6. △   7. ▱

8. ⬠   9. ◺   10. ◇   11. ▷

12. In the space below and using an appropriate tool, create a shape with parallel lines containing no right angles.

13. In the space below and using an appropriate tool, create a shape with parallel lines and no more than two right angles.

14. Can a shape have perpendicular lines and have no right angle?

Source for standard: NGA & CCSSO, 2010b.

Figure 1.5: Sample mathematics assessment—classification of shapes.

To illustrate the point made earlier, let's visit questions one through three. They play an important foundational role. If the assessment started with question four and mistakes were made, knowing how to respond to the errors would require additional research. From a data analysis perspective, those foundational questions let the evaluator know if students understand the vocabulary necessary to accurately respond to the remainder of the questions.

Students are required to apply their knowledge and skills by interpreting and responding to questions twelve through fourteen. There is an additional level of complexity to these questions. Correct answers indicate the ability to demonstrate a deeper understanding of the targets.

Evaluating data should include a consideration as to what constitutes a lack of understanding and what is a minor error. It is the lack of understanding that requires a response, including additional instruction, guided practice, and assessment. The student is best to correct a minor error. When a student can recognize and correct his or her error, an additional intervention by the teacher is likely unnecessary.

A direct connection between the standard and lesson targets will help to identify the response needed should a student have difficulty. When foundational skills that are necessary to successfully applying understanding are included on the assessments as illustrated in figure 1.3 (page 14) and figure 1.5, the data clearly indicate where students are struggling. The questions help to identify not only that students are struggling, but why they are having difficulty. Are they confused with a foundational skill, or does applying the skill cause the problem? Depending on which is the source of confusion, the response to data would be quite different.

With each example, the pattern has been the same. Foundational questions are at the beginning, followed by tasks that serve to apply knowledge and skills. The purpose doesn't vary. If we want to accurately respond to student misunderstandings, we need to have confidence that we have pinpointed the reason for the misunderstanding.

Linking Student Response, the Question, and the Expected Response

Consider what action is required in order to correctly identify what students need when an error occurs. Although the answer key provides the expected response on many assessments, it doesn't supply enough information. Whether a company-designed assessment or one created internally, the answer key is usually just a start to evaluating the assessment. Often the answer alone will not provide the data we require to determine an effective response.

Consider the example in figure 1.6 (page 18). The figure shows three examples, none of which have the correct answer. If teachers use an answer key alone to evaluate the problem, each would be marked wrong. A quick analysis will identify that each response is wrong for a different reason. Regardless of the subject of the assessment, the process provides the information needed in order to respond to student misunderstandings. This mathematics example illustrates the importance

Example Assessment Results—Reviewing the Error		
Example 1	Example 2	Example 3
344 × 42 ── 688 + 1376 ── 2064	344 × 42 ── 688 + 13320 ── 14008	344 × 42 ── 688 + 13760 ── 14428

Figure 1.6: Sample assessment results—reviewing the error.

of process analysis. However, process analysis is not unique to mathematics and should be considered in every content area.

A glance at example one reveals that the student didn't consider place value. Instead of multiplying 344 by 40, he or she multiplied by the number 4. This response requires a reminder and practice with the place value associated with multiplication. This is a process issue, and the student will likely repeat it if not corrected.

The student who completed the problem labeled example two made an error with a basic fact. The student multiplied four by four and identified the product as twelve. In this case, the student might be asked to check the facts and recalculate the answer. The process used for multiplication is correct, so the error is easily fixed and doesn't constitute a misunderstanding.

Example three illustrates a simple addition error. Eight plus six is equal to fourteen, not twelve. As with example two, the student needs to check over the basic facts and correct the answer. The student knows the process. This error is also a quick fix and likely requires no additional response.

To best evaluate student assessment results, the expected response should include the answer and the process. Often the answer is a process as in figure 1.3 (page 14) because students are expected to write an introductory paragraph. When the process is the task assigned in the assessment, a rubric or checklist used for evaluation is beneficial. These tools will help students best illustrate their response and will provide feedback should the response not meet expectations. The intent of the feedback is to communicate aspects of the quality of student performance and modify student thinking to improve learning. For the feedback to be effective, students should see the connection of the feedback to their performance. Feedback should always be presented within a time frame during which it can impact student success; students understand it and have a desire to use it to grow in their performance (Renshaw, Baroutsis, Van Kraayenoord, Goos, & Dole, 2013).

Clarity of the desired outcome assists greatly during the data analysis. The goal is to identify a comprehensive expectation of quality. With a heightened level of clarity, the student response can be compared with the expectation, gaps identified, and next steps established. Although we have been discussing the role of the teacher in assessment analysis, consider that the student can be an active partner in evaluating areas of challenge as well as establishing next steps to strengthen abilities. The partnership between teacher and students can increase the effectiveness of any steps deemed necessary when responding to assessment data.

Connecting Assessment, Data Analysis, and Data Response

Now that assessment structure has been associated with supplying meaningful data, let's consider the connection between assessment, data analysis, and data response. Data provide facts that, through discussion and interpretation, evolve into information. It is in the information that a response is identified.

Making meaning of assessment results gives us the power to respond in a purposeful and relevant way. If students are to grow and perform at expected levels of success, our goal is to analyze current performance and impact student understanding by responding to student need. There is data, which in and of itself has no meaning; there is information, which is data that has meaning through analysis; and there is information, which is useful data, analyzed and connected to action. The latter is what we prefer (Mandinach, Honey, & Light, 2006).

Data analysis often benefits from viewing and reviewing data from a variety of perspectives. Common assessments provide the opportunity to have multiple minds analyzing and making meaning of classroom, grade-level, or department data. Various viewpoints generate multiple potential responses. Teams working together can create opportunities to respond to results in multiple ways. Teams can also generate ideas to support and share students when remediation or reteaching is necessary. For example, a team may group or regroup students into different teachers' classrooms to provide focused instruction by concept or standard. Each teacher works on specific areas of instruction rather than all teachers duplicating efforts within their classroom with only their original group of students.

Teams or teachers should take care not to use data to only confirm assumptions but also to challenge beliefs and generate new ideas. When there is a suspicion that students are struggling for a specific reason, review assessment results and evaluate to determine if that is truly a possibility while also looking for additional potential causes. The ability to accurately identify the causes for misconceptions is essential for a successful response. Consider going to a doctor with a specific symptom, perhaps an earache in the left ear. The doctor will likely check both ears and your throat to look for additional surrounding causes to your illness. The purpose is to treat the causes and eliminate the illness. In the case of assessment analysis, we look at the error and identify causes that could be foundational to student understanding leading to the error.

When responding to data, teachers can group students flexibly when similar misunderstandings occur. This allows students to be grouped by need and is an efficient way to meet student needs. As they consider grouping students according to need, teachers should take care when placing students in temporary groups while responding to current needs. Long-term ability grouping has been shown to widen the achievement gap and should be avoided. Flexible grouping should occur over the short term to meet immediate needs or respond to assessment results. Long-term groups typically last for units or chapters of study, semesters, or full years. Flexible grouping, when structured with a dedicated beginning and ending time frame, can expand opportunities for students (Datnow, 2017).

Should the occasion arise where data indicate a lack of understanding by the majority of students, it is likely that the assessment came too early in the learning process. Take a step back. Present additional learning experiences. Provide opportunities for practice. Continue to offer feedback. Assessing the students again will result in evidence associated with an increased level of success.

To make the best use of data, always consider, in advance, how data will be collected and reported. Several suggestions for reporting and analyzing data are included in chapter 3.

Linking Data to Action

As we view student assessment results, it is clear that our goal is to react to misunderstandings and meet student needs. Data also challenge us to analyze and reflect on the impact of the teaching methods and strategies used because data provide us with evidence to determine the effectiveness of those strategies. Plans can include the use of methods that have proven to result in the greatest levels of student success.

To turn data into action, consider the following questions.

- Why do we want to distinguish between what is essential for a student to understand, compared to what is nice to know?

- When correcting an assessment, how does an analysis of errors help determine the types of response necessary to meet student needs?

- How can working as a team help turn data into actionable information?

CHAPTER 2

Creating a Structure to Support Data Consistency for Common Assessments

The purpose of this chapter is to define specific aspects associated with common assessment, not to include question design, but rather structural design. Even if the assessment is not intended to be common, this chapter highlights important considerations prior to implementing any assessments intended for individual classroom use. Why is this important? Because if aspects of quality assessment design are incorporated into the build, the result will be data that are both meaningful and reliable. We want to review quality dependable data; therefore, we construct assessments that will result in accurate and actionable information.

Common assessment refers to any content or set of standards evaluated in a similar fashion. The assessment is *common* because at least two teachers use or implement it in two or more classes. In addition, collaborative teams administer, score, and review these assessments (Ainsworth, 2007). In collaborative teams, educators work together and take collective responsibility for each student's success (DuFour, DuFour, Eaker, Many, & Mattos, 2016). Further, "*collaboration* represents a systematic process in which teachers work together interdependently in order to *impact* their classroom practice in ways that will lead to better results for their students, for their team, and for their school" (DuFour et al., 2016, p. 12). Therefore, the purpose of a common assessment is to evaluate student understanding in an effort to respond and improve performance.

Typically, assessment includes four steps: (1) the assessment design, (2) the implementation, (3) the data review, and (4) the data response. Although all steps are important, for the focus of this book, the response is the most crucial step. It has the potential of impacting teaching strategies, classroom activities, and student performance. Without the response, change can be random or accidental. Teachers benefit from their ability to analyze and evaluate learning while including both the contextual and situational factors. Connecting the information gathered through data analysis and understanding the impact on learning will result in subsequent actions directly intended to boost student performance (Guerriero, n.d.). The purpose of common assessments, then, is not only to generate common data, but to collectively and collaboratively respond to the data.

To generate effective actions associated with common assessment results, it is preferable to review aspects of the assessment that could unintentionally impact or skew data. Such aspects could result in faulty or misguided conclusions. We want the data to be pure, comparable, and actionable.

The sections that follow will highlight points that impact data. First, assessment structure and design are instrumental in providing data that will lead to actionable data. Second, when implementing common assessments, the word *common* refers to more than the assessment questions and structure. It includes aspects of the implementation process that can impact the data. Lastly, whether analyzing data individually or as a team, the goal is to obtain actionable, accurate information.

Structure and Test Design

When designing a common assessment, it is not always possible to have identical content, because we don't always have a situation in which more than one teacher is responsible for teaching the same content. That doesn't need to deter anyone from creating a common assessment. When the assessment is intended to be common, we will work from an understanding that the standards identified for the assessment are common, but the content is not necessarily identical. When an assessment is being built for a single grade level, learning the same standards, in the same content area, the assessment can be exactly the same. This promotes comparability of response data. In some instances, identical content is not always immediately apparent, but it certainly is possible. For example, a school may have only one class at each grade level. In this case, the assessment may be based on different content, but the common assessment can be built on similar standards. The students, for example, may be assessed on their understanding and identification of theme, but the reading selections used may differ because the assessment is given at different grade levels.

The challenge is not only to evaluate standards and content, but to assess students in such a way that the results can lead directly back to the methods used when teaching the concepts being assessed. It is then possible to scaffold learning and adjust teaching strategies to effectively meet needs both prior to and after the assessment is administered (Renshaw et al., 2013). As with any assessment of learning, we certainly want to know what students understand and misunderstand, but most importantly, we want the data to lead to a clear and accurate response. Being conscious of what students need to know, do, and apply as well as being keenly aware of teaching methods will lead to a well-rounded response.

Figure 2.1 provides an example of a cross-grade level common assessment. Although at each grade level the standard becomes a bit more sophisticated, a common assessment can be based on the group of standards. Teachers can then discuss student progression on the standards, provide insights into student challenges, and discuss strategies to teach the standards. All will support impactful responses to data collected on a common assessment.

Text Type and Purposes
RL.3.1 Ask and answer questions to demonstrate understanding of a text, referring explicitly to the text as the basis for the answers.
RL.4.1 Refer to details and examples in a text when explaining what the text says explicitly and when drawing inferences from the text.
RL.5.1 Quote accurately from a text when explaining what the text says explicitly and when drawing inferences from the text.

Source for standards: NGA & CCSSO, 2010a.

Figure 2.1: Example of cross-grade level commonalities—text type and purposes.

The goal of any assessment is to have students perform in a way that is reflective of their understanding. We want to make sure that the questions or tasks are clear and understandable and will illustrate effectively student knowledge and skills. Quality test design assists in accurate, reliable data.

When designing assessments individually or with a team, consider some of the hints provided in *Raising the Rigor* (Depka, 2017). The Definite Dozen provides an overview of what to consider before and during the assessment design process (see table 2.1, page 26). Practices for Traditional Test Formats gives a series of hints that will help students be better able to respond to the assessment as a result of the structural design (see table 2.2, page 27).

Formulating questions and tasks is an integral part of the assessment design process. When the desire is to accurately measure student understanding, teachers or teams review the assessment with an eye on validity and reliability. Do the questions or tasks measure the standards, learning targets, and contents that they

Table 2.1: Assessment Design Considerations—The Definite Dozen

Consideration	Additional Information
1. All questions align to one or more standards.	Selecting specific standards that the assessment addresses dictates the types of questions to ask and the skills on which to focus. If content is not specific in the standards, identify the focus.
2. Assessment has a clear focus, topic, or purpose.	Identify a clear purpose. What will this assessment accomplish? What do we want to know? The identified purpose is reflective of the standards we have selected.
3. All questions and statements are clearly written and in full sentences (except completion items).	Questions should be clear and free from any confusion that could cause students to answer incorrectly.
4. Assessment contains higher-level thinking opportunities.	The purpose is to ensure that students have a true understanding of the concepts and can apply them to new or unique situations.
5. Questions match the intended targets and content.	Consider the desired outcome of the question and match it to the question design. A task, project, or open-ended question can be beneficial when asking students to analyze information.
6. Two to three questions address the same skill to ensure students can repeat the expected performance.	If students are able to apply a skill and get the correct answer once, can they repeat it? A second similar question will provide an additional opportunity, and a third can validate if the skill can be repeated at least two of three times.
7. Assessment provides opportunities for students to apply knowledge and skills to realistic situations.	When students are given the opportunity to apply what they know to real-life situations, they better understand the purpose of what they are learning.
8. Point value is clear for each question if questions have varied point levels.	When questions have different values, identifying the value helps students to know where additional time and effort may be required.
9. Success criteria are defined. (What do students need to do to earn a 1, 2, 3, or 4?)	When different values are assigned to questions, students will perform better if they understand the requirements to achieve the levels.
10. A rubric is available for essay and performance-based items.	A rubric provides descriptors of quality. The rubric clearly defines the level of achievement required to earn a top performance.
11. A system is in place to collect, record, and analyze data.	The goal of the assessment is to evaluate the strengths and challenge areas of students. Have a defined way to collect, record, and analyze the data.
12. Successful completion of the assessment will show that students know and understand the concepts being tested.	After writing the assessment, compare the finished product to the intended targets. If students do well on the assessment, will that also indicate that they have the expected knowledge and skills?

Source: Depka, 2017, p. 39.

Table 2.2: Practices for Traditional Test Formats

Consideration	Additional Information
1. Assessment is typed.	This is most often the practice, but sometimes when pressed for time, we might decide to handwrite an assessment. This can make it more difficult for some students to read, thereby making it less possible to answer the question correctly.
2. Assessment has clearly written directions for all sections.	In order for students to be certain of expectations, directions are needed. Consider also going through the directions orally with students. If expectations are clear, students have a better chance at success.
3. Assessment contains a variety of types of questions and no more than ten of any one type.	We want students to experience success. We don't want the style of questions to confuse students. Giving multiple formats will provide students the opportunity to demonstrate their knowledge with less chance that the question type will impede their progress.
4. Length of the test is geared to fit within a single class period and takes no more than about two to four minutes multiplied by the students' age.	The goal of the assessment is to get the best student performance possible. We don't want fatigue to play a role in results. Assessing more frequently or spacing the assessment out over a few days can also help control the fatigue factor. (Example: 8-year-olds times 2–4 minutes = 16–32 minutes)
5. Assessment provides ample space for student responses.	When answer space is present, students can rely on the questions in front of them without being required to transfer questions or problems to a new document. They can concentrate on what is being asked without the distraction of answering elsewhere. When the test is returned to them, they will also have access to the original questions and not only their response.
6. Questions are arranged from simple to complex.	This practice can help build confidence in students. It can also help scaffold understanding. From a data perspective, it will allow responses to be analyzed to determine whether or not students had the basics that were needed to apply to more complex questions.
7. Questions are written at a reading level appropriate to the students.	When questions contain vocabulary or phrasing that students don't understand, it will impact their ability to respond accurately. Questions needn't be simplified, but reading level doesn't hinder performance.
8. Assessment includes choices. (Optional)	If used, construct choices to evaluate the same knowledge and skills. The application might vary, but the result should provide evidence of the students' level of understanding on the skill or topic. For example, if the goal is to have students identify the theme of a story, the following options could apply. Option one: Explain the theme of the story and provide evidence and justification for your opinion. Option two: Create an illustration of the theme providing evidence and detail from the story. Explain how your drawing is representative of the theme.

Source: Depka, 2017, pp. 40–41.

are intended to measure (validity)? Are the questions and tasks capable of getting the same results consistently throughout classrooms and over time (reliability)?

Assessment implementation goes beyond development of the questions. Considering format can provide students with an assessment architecture that assists in providing their best response. For example, if students can respond directly on the assessment, they can concentrate on their answer, which will be conveniently located near the question on the assessment. If students are not responsible for transferring questions to another location, they can concentrate on deciphering the meaning of the task, not on copying the task. We want the students to concentrate on their performance. Creating an easy-to-use format will support students, not distract them. We want students to put all of their time and effort into demonstrating their expertise.

Consider the assessment's format and its potential impact on student performance. The teacher cannot always control the format; however, he or she should take into account its impact when analyzing the results should they differ from previous performance on similar concepts. For example, according to FutureEd (2017), a think tank associated with Georgetown University, students perform better on pencil-and-paper tests than they do on those that are computer based. However, over time, the result discrepancies fade between the two styles of testing.

Directions and Common Implementation

Think about the work that goes into creating a writing assessment. Prompts are discussed and agreed upon. Rubrics are generated. Rubrics are tested to ensure inter-rater reliability. This is no small task. It would be unfortunate if the results of all of this work were not as reliable as possible due to differences during the implementation phase.

The word *common* also encompasses the need for a common set of expectations. Discussing directions with colleagues prior to the assessment benefits the collaborative team of teachers, the students, and the quality of the results. If the assessment is being used in a single classroom, attention should also be paid to clarity and consistency of directions.

Consistency of administration increases uniformity, resulting in data that are more likely to be comparable. Let's first consider the directions. The prompts and rubrics provide the contents of the assessment. However, if we stop there, each classroom potentially could provide different directions, a different process, and a structure that is unique to that classroom. Scripted directions assist in a uniform process.

In order to ensure a common understanding of expectations, directions for each section of the assessment should be discussed, agreed on, and put in writing. Write directions that will be read to and by all students prior to giving the assessment. Consider the directions to be a script that all teachers will have available and follow. This will increase consistency across classrooms and among schools. Figure 2.2 provides an example. Review the rubric the week prior to the assessment. Regular use of this rubric will increase the likelihood of student success.

Script: Exact wording to use with students

The piece you are about to create is part of our grade-level writing assessment. Please put forth your best effort. Teachers will use the results of the assessment to evaluate the writing abilities of all students in the district and to help make decisions about the strengths and challenges of our students. You will receive your results along with feedback on strengths and suggestions for improving your writing.

You will have two class periods to complete the writing assessment. First create an outline, then a first draft. You will then edit the document and create a finished product.

On day one, you will be working only on the outline, draft, and edits.

On day two, you will be given paper to complete the final product. All of your work will be collected on day one and returned to you on day two.

If you choose, you can use a dictionary or thesaurus for your work.

The learning targets for this assessment are listed on the directions I have given to you. The learning targets are as follows.

- Convey ideas and information clearly.
- Introduce topic clearly.
- Group related information in paragraphs.
- Develop topics with facts, definitions, quotes, and details.
- Link ideas using verbs and phrases.
- Use language and vocabulary that inform the topic.
- Provide a concluding statement.

The scoring rubric is attached as well. Let's review it now. (Briefly review rubric.)

Are there any questions?

Figure 2.2: Sample directions for writing common assessments.

The directions provide clarity and focus. The intent is to give students not only the same directions, but to offer a complete set of instructions and define the targets of the assessment. Both oral and written directions are beneficial to the students. Written directions give students the opportunity to revisit the expectations as needed. Both the process and content are clear in the minds of the teachers and the students. The process supports the likelihood of quality, reliable data.

Common implementation calls for additional considerations. The thought process to resolve implementation questions is not time consuming, but helpful in the smooth operation of any common assessment. Figure 2.3 lists a series of questions. Consider developing a common understanding and practice for each when implementing any common assessment. Many responses will become common practice within your learning community and will usually need only verification, not discussion. These same responses can also be beneficial to single classroom assessments.

Category	Questions to Consider	Common Understanding and Practice
Time Frame of the Assessment	• How long should the assessment take? • Is this a class period? A number of minutes?	
Additional Time Option	• Because we don't want time to be a factor, additional time should be considered, but how much can you reasonably support? • When will students be provided the additional time?	
Assessment Date	• What if all teachers want to give the assessment on the same day? • What day should the assessment be given? (Often an option within a series of dates allows for more flexibility but can cause concerns about student discussion of assessment contents prior to taking the assessment. Teachers can remedy this by creating different forms. It is also not a concern if the assessment is task oriented, requiring students to demonstrate understanding beyond factual information.)	
Directions	• Will directions be given in writing and orally? • How much additional explanation is allowable?	
Supportive Tools	• Can a dictionary be used? • Will students have access to technology? • Will a graphic organizer be available? • Will tools specific to the subject area be available (for example, calculator, notes, text, and so on)? • Can questions be read to students? • What methods will be used to differentiate the assignment?	

Category	Questions to Consider	Common Understanding and Practice
Teacher Responsibilities During the Assessment	• Will teachers be actively observing students? • Will teachers be watching students whose minds wander to help them refocus on the task? • Will teachers provide any guidance if students ask for assistance? • Will teachers provide any guidance to students they observe doing things incorrectly?	
Time Allotment for Assessment	• Will there be times and locations open to all students taking the assessment to provide equal opportunity for test completion?	
Scoring of Assessment	• Is a common scoring system in place for assessment evaluation? • Is there an existing rubric to use to score tasks, or does one need to be identified or designed?	
Data Collection and Organization	• How will you format the data so that, when meeting with colleagues, they are easily comparable? • Will you color-code the data? Have the colors been identified?	
Meeting to Evaluate the Data	• Will everyone be expected to have the data in the agreed-upon format? • What questions will you ask about the data?	
Acting on the Results	• How will action items be identified? • What will be used to distinguish between optional and essential actions? • Are there ways to share students so as not to duplicate efforts, but make an efficient use of teachers' time? • In what time frame will actions be completed?	
Other	• Are there other components of the assessment to discuss prior to implementation to support consistency and accuracy of results?	

Figure 2.3: Common assessment implementation considerations.

*Visit **go.SolutionTree.com/assessment** for a free reproducible version of this figure.*

Proficiency

What do we want to be confident that students know, can do, and are able to apply? Reviewing the questions in advance will provide us with the opportunity to define quality for student performance on each item. In some cases, there may be a single correct answer. With other answers, a point identification system or rubric is necessary to evaluate the quality and accuracy of the response. Prior to the assessment, this work will clarify what exactly is needed to indicate the student is performing at a proficient level.

As mentioned previously, frequent assessments provide us with ongoing data regarding student progress. We identify misunderstandings early before they turn into gaps. When assessing often, the length of the assessment itself varies. We may provide just a few questions when the concepts have been tested on multiple occasions and students have mostly experienced success. Repeated assessment ensures that students remember and continue to respond accurately to the concepts determined essential, yet extensive repeated testing is not necessary. If we establish proficiency expectations prior to the assessment, we are more likely to accurately identify need and less likely to overidentify the need for an intervention.

Let's use figure 2.4 as an example of a brief assessment that is intended to determine whether students can recognize and use nouns appropriately. A quick review shows us that if students are able to recognize the majority of nouns in part one, they know what a noun is. We also pay attention to whether they also recognize proper nouns. If students are able to complete parts two and three, they are also able to choose nouns on their own and use them in a sentence. In other words, they can recognize (part one), generate (part two), and create and identify them (part three). Errors throughout the assessment indicate misunderstandings, which the student needs to correct with assistance from the teacher as necessary. However, if students can complete the majority with limited error, it is an indication that they understand. Trying to place a percentage is difficult on a short assessment of three to five questions, for example. Rather, select what determines proficiency. It may be that, in brief assessments, demonstrating understanding two out of three times is acceptable.

Determining proficiency is crucial to set the stage as to whether or not a response to data is required. A percentage doesn't tell the story. Repeated, accurate student performance provides evidence of competence. The point that the teacher needs to consider is the number of repetitions students need to display competence on an assessment.

Consider the difficulty from using a percentage. On a quick check assessment, students might be given only three opportunities to perform a skill, and in that

---

Part 1: Directions—Circle the nouns in the following sentences.

1. The little dog ran through the park jumping and barking happily.

2. Jeremy hit the baseball hard, but Jenny was able to catch it.

3. Rain caused the picnic to be postponed.

Part 2: Directions—In each space, write a noun of your choice.

1.

2.

3.

4.

5.

Part 3: Directions—Create a sentence of your own including at least two nouns. Circle the nouns in your sentence.

Figure 2.4: Short assessment example—identification of nouns.

case, a 66 percent can be very acceptable, especially when the error indicates a simple mistake but not confusion as to the process the student used to arrive at a correct response. The goal is to connect proficiency to student performance on each section of the assessment tied to the concepts being assessed within. Pinpoint what students need to show. Decide what will give you a good level of confidence that students understand. Evaluate the concepts being assessed. Determine the number of times a student needs to accurately repeat a performance to determine proficiency. There is no magic number; it is tied to the sophistication of the standards and content being tested. If a student is asked to identify a theme, this skill is repeated throughout the year using multiple pieces of literature and multiple assessments. When the student is being assessed on his or her ability to multiply two-digit numbers, for example, determine the number of accurate repetitions needed to have confidence the student understands and can implement the procedure. Review and record performance on each section of the assessment to provide informative data, such as the sample assessments later in the chapter.

Establish a match between the concepts assessed and the number of times the performance must be repeated to determine understanding. During assessment design, teachers create a plan that ensures the number of items corresponding to each learning target will be informative. The structure and number of questions assigned to each concept support the intended outcome, which is the ability of students to securely interpret student performance (Vagle, 2015).

When a common assessment is of greater length, determining proficiency by section throughout the assessment in advance is necessary. Pinpoint the intended outcome. Be clear on what a proficient performance looks like. Student performance doesn't impact the identified definition of proficiency. It remains the same. If students struggle, we help them reach proficiency, not lower it. If students excel, we celebrate.

Provide enough detail in the assessment to best identify why errors are caused. Discuss how many times students need to provide an accurate response in order to consider them proficient. If a skill can be demonstrated two of three times, is that enough to know students can duplicate a process? Is more validation required? When asked to apply their understanding, what will an acceptable response look like? Figure 2.5 is an example of a mathematics common assessment. Figure 2.6 (page 36) offers a detailed breakdown of a potential response should students struggle. When reviewing figure 2.5, consider what you believe students would need to show you to inspire confidence that they understand, even if errors are present. This can be dependent on grade level and time of year. It is likely that if students can complete the majority of the first three sections, they have a solid understanding of the content.

I find that it is sometimes counterintuitive to realize that proficiency does not mean perfection. Instead, it is the demonstration of understanding at a level that provides the evidence showing students can perform repeatedly and accurately enough. Their performance gives us confidence that students can duplicate a display of understanding and ensure that it can be repeated over time.

How many times does a student need to repeat his or her performance to ensure competence? The answer is key. Keep this in mind throughout any assessment design or evaluation process. If using company-designed assessments, review the assessment with this purpose in mind. Repeated performance can cause fatigue. More is not necessarily better; it's just more. Determine the *just right* amount.

Planning for assessment implementation should include the identification of some type of calibration process where teachers come to consensus about the goals and expectations on the assessment (Kerr, Marsh, Ikemoto, Darilek, & Barney, 2006). Points, scales, rubrics, and any other methods of scoring should be clear in advance of implementing a common assessment. Clarity will support the ability to accurately make data comparisons.

Write the name of the number in words.

1. 346 _____three hundred forty-six_____

2. 907 _____nine hundred seven_____

3. 1,258 _____one thousand, two hundred fifty-eight_____

4. 7,012 _____seven thousand, twelve_____

5. 13,000 _____thirteen thousand_____

6. 345,202 _three hundred forty-five thousand, two hundred two_

7. 3,231,421 _three million, two hundred thirty-one thousand, four hundred twenty-one_

8. 12,000,021 _____twelve million, twenty-one_____

Write the number using numerals.

9. Four hundred fifty-two _____452_____

10. Eight hundred one _____801_____

11. Two thousand, four hundred twenty-nine _____2,429_____

12. Twelve thousand, one _____12,001_____

13. Two million, four thousand, two hundred forty-seven _____2,004,247_____

14. Two hundred ninety-four million, twenty-seven thousand

_____294,027,000_____

Place a sign between the numbers to create a correct comparison. Use <, >, or =.

15. 9 _>_ 7

16. 22 _<_ 167

17. 429 _=_ 429

18. 1,345 _<_ 1,354

19. 20,007 _>_ 19,986

20. 14,789 _<_ 150,000

Answer the questions about the following problem.

21. The food store manager ordered nine thousand, forty-eight oranges and 9,048 bananas. Which fruit was ordered in the greater quantity ordered? How do you know?

Figure 2.5: Sample grade 4 mathematics—numbers and operations in base-ten common assessment with answers.

4.NBT.2: Generalize place value understanding for multidigit whole numbers. Read and write multi-digit whole numbers using base-ten numerals, number names, and expanded form. Compare two multidigit numbers based on meanings of the digits in each place, using >, =, and < symbols to record the results of comparisons.

Skill Assessed	Response If Student Is Unsuccessful	Associated Test Items
Read three-digit numbers.	If students are unable to complete these items, they will likely be unsuccessful with the assessment. Reteaching using place value charts will benefit the students.	1–2
Read four- to six-digit numbers.	Analyze the errors. If there are mistakes, it may be due to students not understanding the meaning of the comma, or they may be struggling with the presence of a zero.	3–8
Read seven- to nine-digit numbers.		
Write three-digit numbers.	These items are included to verify that a student is able to read and write three-digit numbers. If errors are made in future problems, it is likely that the student struggles with place value of larger numbers.	9–10
Write four- to six-digit numbers.	Incorrect responses indicate that the student is struggling with the thousands place and needs a review.	11–12
Write seven- to nine-digit numbers.	Incorrect responses indicate that the student is struggling with the millions place and needs a review.	13–14
Compare multi-digit numbers using <, >, = signs.	These are included to ensure that students understand each symbol and can place it correctly. It is likely they recognize the larger number, or if numbers are equal, so a mistake is probably due to not understanding the symbol direction.	15–17
	If students have a correct use of signs in 15–17, but are unable to complete 18–20, they may have difficulty with visual discrimination or with place value. Have students place the two numbers beneath each other, aligning commas, to see if they can determine the correct response. If they can, the problem is not place value; if they are unsuccessful, review place value of larger numbers.	18–20
	The purpose of this problem is to determine if students can compare written numbers with numerals. It also requires students to explain how they arrived at their response.	21

Source for standard: NGA & CCSSO, 2010b.

Figure 2.6: Sample item response analysis—numbers and operations in base-ten common assessment.

Individual and Team Data Analysis and Action

Summative and formative data both serve a purpose when determining how to respond to results. Any action that serves to support student achievement in an appropriate and meaningful way should be considered (Mandinach et al., 2006).

On occasion, terminology connected with assessment gets confusing. To simplify, consider it important to analyze and respond to all assessment, no matter the descriptor. Let's not let the adjectives associated with the assessment complicate matters. Is it formative, summative, a quick check, a chapter test, a unit assessment, a state test, a common assessment, or a district assessment? The goal is to learn from student performance and respond appropriately depending on the purpose of the assessment.

Let's consider purpose. If the goal of the assessment is to determine whether or not students are understanding concepts throughout the lesson or chapter, quickly checking the accuracy of performance is necessary. These assessments are intended to evaluate small pieces of content or standards. Students complete the typically brief assessment, we review it, and we take action as necessary to clarify understanding and correct errors. This type of check for understanding is typically done in single classrooms and instituted as needed, although it can be planned in advance with a team of teachers providing instruction in the same content area. The student and teacher alike gain confidence when performances show the desired level of competence.

Cumulative assessments also require analysis and action. This type of assessment combines two or more learning targets or concepts and can be used formatively or summatively depending on the identified purpose. Prior to a cumulative assessment, it is recommended that quick checks be performed for any content important to student success before moving to combining multiple pieces of content, targets, or standards. These short assessments result in the opportunity to clear up any misunderstandings and provide additional practice as necessary to prepare students for a more successful experience as more content is added. The quick checks increase our level of confidence that, when a more cumulative evaluation is enacted, there is a likelihood of great success.

Evaluating cumulative results requires action if there is confusion about concepts or processes that are crucial to immediate or future success. The action is an exact response to the source of the confusion. Whole-class misunderstandings require reteaching of the concepts, additional practice, and reassessment. Individual needs are supported through the same process. The more accountability that teachers can place on students being engaged in their own learning, the greater the chance of long-term success. Student engagement promotes interest. Students become more self-reliant and interested in their learning (Taylor & Parsons, 2011). The closer in time that the response is to the source of the confusion, the greater the probability of a quick fix to the problem.

School, district, and state assessments are often delayed in response and serve a different purpose. The goal of most is to evaluate student performance on a cumulative set of skills and demonstrations of understanding. Team data analysis often follows this type of assessment. A direct classroom-level response is typically not possible as it is too far removed from the teaching of the content. However, these results provide guidance for future teaching, planning, and implementation as a school or district. Determine those areas deemed essential for future success. Pinpoint procedures and applications of understanding that lead to increased grade-level performance. A comparison between challenge areas and grade-level curriculum will assist in identifying skills, concepts, and procedures that require additional time, resources, and quick checks throughout the time of teaching. Although assessment data that are analyzed at the end of the school year are not likely to help the students that year, a response at future grade levels will enhance performance at the next level.

Classroom data analysis by individual teachers is different. It happens on a daily basis. Analysis throughout the hour, the lessons, the week, the chapter, and the unit provides evidence that supports next steps. Student confusion becomes clear, and responses are closely tied to demonstrating the misunderstanding. Reviewing the source of confusion results in a clear path to next steps.

When implementing common assessments, set a date and time for data analysis in advance to ensure that the entire group will be available for the discussion. Each teacher can review their individual and class data in advance, so they are fully prepared for the group discussion. The analysis can include comparison between concepts assessed. Comparisons can also be made of results among classrooms in an effort to analyze student performance and share ideas. Collective responses to the data can be identified, and actions planned and implemented. Chapter 3 will highlight various ways to collect, report on, and interpret data. Chapter 4 will provide multiple suggestions on planning and implementing the response to data.

Data analysis and action is an ongoing process and should be thought of as a constant cycle. Checks for understanding scheduled regularly throughout a unit of time are beneficial. Errors in understanding are quickly rectified. We don't wait until the end of a chapter or unit to find that students are struggling. Progress tests can provide data, yet additional sources like assignments, projects,

performances, conversations, and observations can give up-to-the minute information on which to act (Marsh, Pane, & Hamilton, 2006). Although some may
not be considered formal assessments, they all provide formative data.

Assessment author Rick Stiggins (2004) states:

> Classroom assessments provide a continuous flow of evidence of
> student mastery of the classroom-level learning targets that lead
> over time to attainment of the desired achievement standards.
> As assessments for learning, they inform instructional decisions
> along the way to success. (p. 26)

Decisions are made in the classroom on a daily basis, and they are critical.
Collecting student performance evidence is directly related to the level of success
a student can experience (Stiggins, 2004).

Figure 2.7 (page 40) provides a picture of a pattern of assessment that assists in
early and effective responses to student need. Imagine the figure to be four small
spinning pinwheels attached to a large pinwheel.

The small pinwheels, labeled *target, teach, test*, indicate the process to identify
the unit targets essential to student success, determine the best strategies to teach
the learning targets, and then assess regularly to check for progress on the lessons.
As a normal part of the assessment cycle, data are analyzed and acted on, and the
cycle continues. These small pinwheels revolve around the inner circle, which is
a cumulative representation of the learning goals encompassed in the entire unit
of study. The shorter, more frequent assessments have a narrow focus, the result
of which provides clear direction toward next steps in reteaching, if necessary. An
outcome of the continuous progress checks includes a greater sense of confidence
in students and a feeling that success on the cumulative assessment is not only
possible, but probable. Because misunderstandings are corrected along the way, it
is highly likely that only limited errors will occur on the cumulative assessment,
and responding to the data will be a comfortable, condensed venture. When a
variety of data are collected and analyzed on an ongoing basis, multiple times
throughout any unit of study, equal attention must be given to data analysis and
action (Marsh et al., 2006). It's not about the data; it's about what we do with
the data.

The teamwork involved in implementing common assessment needs coordina-
tion, forethought, and time. Discussions, the identification of common understanding regarding assessment and evaluation, collaboration around data, and
actions responding to the data are all part of the needs associated when implementing common assessments. Teamwork helps us to learn, grow, and share ideas

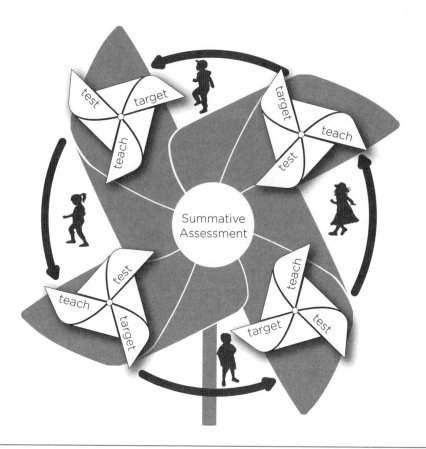

Figure 2.7: Response to assessment—the wheel that works.

and strategies. Collectively we become better at what we do because we expand our own knowledge and skills due to the team collaboration.

Individual responsibilities are apparent in the assessment process as well. In our classroom, we respond to the needs of students by committing to regularly implementing a variety of checks for understanding. This can include anything from observation, to conversation, to assignments, to more structured assessments based on a limited number of standards. The analysis and response to our findings support students' enhanced and continued success.

Linking Data to Action

With any assessment, the goal is to collect reliable information about student understanding. Content should not surprise students, because we want them to be prepared and perform at their best. The assessment is intended to contain concepts previously taught unless it is used as a pretest. Students have had ample opportunity to practice the learning outcomes prior to being assessed summatively. Useable data will result. The assessments will provide a meaningful source of information. "Assessments provide teachers with specific guidance in their efforts to improve the quality of their teaching by helping identify what they taught well and what needs work" (Guskey, 2007, p. 18).

To turn data into action, consider the following questions.

- How do assessment structure and design impact the ability to gain quality data?

- How do you determine how many times a student needs to display a skill or standard in order to demonstrate proficiency?

- When analyzing assessment results, in what ways is the analysis of individual responses helpful in determining how to respond to the data?

CHAPTER 3

Visualizing and Interpreting Data With an Eye on Action

Positive outcomes in student learning are increased when teachers have the ability to interpret data and reflect on the impact of their teaching and instructional practices. The connection between teaching and learning becomes clear, and a response to data is understandable (Hong & Lawrence, 2011).

In education, we are no longer deciding whether to incorporate data into decision making, but instead, we are deciding how to best incorporate data (Protheroe, 2009). As educators, we understand that using data is necessary; the step we are now engaged in is finding meaningful and effective ways to use data in the classroom. Collecting data requires consideration in advance of method and format. Do we have an identified purpose for collecting the data? What specifically will we collect? With what specificity will we record the data? How will we make the results easy to interpret and actionable? Are we sharing the data as a collaborative team? Will that make a difference as to how they are collected and recorded?

Several questions exist, but all have the same answer. Collect, record, and analyze data that will assist in accurately and efficiently responding to student needs on a continuous basis. Data can always be recorded in a similar fashion. Choose what works for you and coincides with any collaborative team expectations in your setting. Keep it simple, yet meaningful.

The data alone will not point to a conclusion, decision, or action. Instead, it is the analysis, the way the individual or team can make sense of the data, that leads to a suitable response. If the data support the need for action, it is we who work to find potential appropriate solutions (Spillane, 2012). The methods we use to collect, display, analyze, and discuss data can support turning data into information.

The incorrect analysis of data can lead to action with no impact, perhaps even harm. This chapter will provide examples of methods to collect and report on data so that they are easy to visualize, interpret, and understand whether working alone or with a team. It will also share ideas of what data can be collected as a school to help determine strengths and challenges. Responses will be shared that support teachers and the school.

To best understand and use data, we can consider some areas that assist in creating a picture of student success that assists determining how we respond. How we organize and display data plays a role in next steps. When developing traditional forms of assessment, design is a consideration as a precursor to data analysis. As a source for valuable information, we also collect and review attitudinal, perception, and reflective data from students. We'll take a look at these areas in the pages that follow.

Data Organization and Display

The organization and display of data are directly related to what we want to know when analyzing them. Our intended outcome drives the method to collect and interpret the data. Assuming that our desired outcome is to collect information about student performance in an effort to identify an appropriate response, we consider in advance the questions we would like the data to answer.

Brainstorm a list of questions that provide insights into learning. Consider the questions that follow as a starting point. What do we want students to know, and how will they use that information? What will we do to assess students, and how will we know that they are proficient? How do students perform compared to the expectation? What can be done to support students and improve achievement? Are the teaching strategies that I'm using having a positive impact on student results? (Protheroe, 2009).

Identifying the questions in advance helps frame ways in which the data are reported. Once identified, questions can be used routinely to analyze results. There is no need to invent new questions with each analysis. However, questions might be added over time when new thoughts arise. The questions asked during data analysis are important to a successful response and outcome. Figure 3.1 includes a set of questions to consider.

The list of questions need not appear daunting. Use questions that get to the heart of the matter. The goal is to have a good understanding of the information and the action that can be gleaned from student results. What are the data telling you? What response, if any, is required?

Questions	Notes or Actions
1. Are there any questions that had incorrect responses by several students?	
2. Are there any concepts that were difficult for several students?	
3. On which concepts were most students successful?	
4. Were there types of questions that students found more difficult?	
5. Were there any questions that multiple students left unanswered?	
6. Were there any surprises in the results?	
7. What misunderstandings need correcting? How will I respond?	
8. Are there any concepts that need reteaching to the class?	
9. Are there any concepts that need reteaching to small groups?	
10. Are there any concepts that need reteaching to individual students?	
11. Are there tasks that I will have students complete to increase their understanding?	
12. How will I engage students, so they can take part in evaluating their strengths and challenges and be a partner in responding to their own needs?	
13. Were the strategies I used effective, and how do I know?	

Figure 3.1: Data-analysis questions.

Traditional Assessment Data

The structure of the assessment can support or complicate a data review. Brief focused assessments evaluating the same learning target are straightforward and uncomplicated to analyze. Assessments with a limited number of targets result in data specific to a defined set of expected learning outcomes.

Figure 3.2 (page 46) is an example of a standards-based English language arts assessment designed to assess the portion of the standard connected to identifying the theme of a story. Students are asked to define *theme*, select a theme based on a book they have just read, and support their choice by providing examples from the text.

RL.4.2: Determine a theme of a story, drama, or poem from details in the text; summarize the text.

1. In your own words, explain the meaning of the word *theme*.
2. Circle the theme that best fits the story.
   a. Love creates a strong bond in families.
   b. Sisters and brothers don't always get along.
   c. Children can get in a lot of trouble.
   d. Bravery is a good quality to have.
3. Give four examples from the text to support the theme you selected. Explain how the examples you have chosen exemplify the theme.

   Example 1:

   Example 2:

   Example 3:

   Example 4:

Source for standard: NGA & CCSSO, 2010a.

Figure 3.2: Sample brief, focused assessment.

The data should coincide with the three sections of this brief assessment. The first section lets the teacher know if students know what a theme is, the second section reveals whether they understand the theme of the book, and the third section highlights the ability of the students to choose details that support the theme.

On the assessment in figure 3.2 students are asked to do only six things all based on theme. To capture the data and make meaning of it, teachers keep a record of any incorrect response on each of the six answers to provide actionable data. A cumulative score alone will not be informative and lead to specific action. If used as a formative assessment or assignment, a grade is likely not attached to it; however, recording the data is essential. To plan and respond appropriately, teachers identify and analyze any misunderstandings. Merely "checking in" an assignment does not provide the information needed to react to student needs. "Checking in" an assignment tells us whether it has been turned in, yet it gives us no information about the quality of performance. Action requires a greater level of detail.

Figure 3.3 gives an example of a quick approach to generate a visual that assists in extracting meaningful information from student performance.

Student Name	Define Theme	Recognize Theme	Support of Theme			
			First	Second	Third	Fourth
Angela				X		
Brody						
Charlene						
Chase	X		X	X	X	X
Denise						
Dominic						
Emily		X				
Jerry			X			
Jessica						
Jimmy						
Jonathan						
Juan			X			
Lauren						
Marco						
Marcy			X			
Michael						
Monica						
Natalie						
Vincent				X		

Figure 3.3: Data display for brief theme assessment featured in figure 3.2.

Figure 3.3 demonstrates two approaches—either shading or using an *X* to record data, yet only one is necessary. An *X* and shading identify incorrect responses. Choose the method that is easiest to see. It's a personal choice.

With any assessment, there should be a limited number of errors if the students were ready to take the assessment. If there appears to be an overwhelming number of errors, it was likely too early to give the assessment. What is overwhelming is particular to the teacher. If there is an obvious sign of confusion on multiple questions, timing is not right. In that case, step back, engage the students in some additional lessons using new strategies, have them practice, and then reassess.

When we review the data in figure 3.3, we look at them in two ways. Horizontally, we can see which students are having difficulty. Chase is clearly having difficulty with understanding and supporting the theme of the story and will need some additional guidance.

Vertically, we identify areas in which the class has misunderstandings. These data show that although there are errors in supporting the theme, everyone in the class with the exception of Chase was able to find at least three pieces of evidence to support the theme. Reteaching is unnecessary as the class understands the concept of supporting theme and is able to provide evidence that they understand. Theme is also addressed throughout the year, and students will have additional opportunities to demonstrate understanding.

It is interesting that, although Emily picked the wrong theme, she was able to support her choice with evidence from the text. In this case, either one of two quick responses is probable. In the first, because Emily could support her choice, is the evidence strong enough to also consider it a theme of the book? If it is, give Emily credit. The second is that Emily can be told the theme and the reasons it is a better choice. She could be asked to find evidence to support the identified theme to help her better understand the reasoning behind the choice. A quick conversation and student follow-through are likely enough to clear up any confusion.

Lengthier summative assessments require preplanning for ease of data analysis. If possible, grouping similar portions of the standard or content being assessed will make analysis less time consuming to organize and evaluate.

Figure 3.4 provides an example of a mathematics assessment that includes multiple concepts associated with understanding fractions and mixed numbers. The concepts are grouped into like procedures which will assist in the recording and analysis of data.

1. Write the fraction that represents the shaded area: _____

Find the missing number to correctly reduce each fraction. Show your work.

2. $\dfrac{24}{32} = \dfrac{3}{}$

3. $\dfrac{6}{9} = \dfrac{2}{}$

Simplify the fractions. Show your work.	
4. $\frac{14}{28} = $ __	5. $\frac{6}{8} = $ __
Find the greatest common factor of each pair of numbers. Show your work.	
6. 16 and 26 ____	7. 18 and 36 ____
Find the least common multiple for each pair of numbers. Show your work.	
8. 6 and 12 ____	9. 12 and 18 ____
Compare the fractions using <, >, or =.	
10. $4\frac{2}{3}$ ◯ $4\frac{5}{9}$	11. $1\frac{7}{8}$ ◯ $1\frac{15}{16}$
12. Jeremy and Jennifer were having a discussion about the fraction of free throws they made during basketball practice. They each took 24 shots. Jeremy said he did better because he made ⅓ of his shots. Jennifer said she did better because she made 8/24 of her shots. Who was correct? How do you know?	

Figure 3.4: Sample mathematics assessment—understanding fractions and mixed numbers.

Student responses to the mathematics assessment can be placed on a grid similar to that in figure 3.3 (page 47). Figure 3.5 (page 50) illustrates the data for this assessment.

Upon viewing figure 3.5, it is apparent that several students are having difficulty finding the greatest common factor of two numbers. Six students were unable to accurately arrive at either answer. This indicates that a response is required. First, we evaluate the strategies to teach GCF and determine how the procedure will be presented to the small group. A brief practice opportunity with immediate feedback is assigned. An additional brief independent exercise is assigned to ensure that students understand and can perform the process. Because their ability to understand and solve this type of problem is essential for success in the next steps in mathematics, it is imperative that students have a solid understanding.

Student Name	Name Fraction (1)	Missing Number (2–3)		Simplify (4–5)		Greatest common factor (GCF) (6–7)		Least common multiple (LCM) (8–9)		Compare (10–11)		Thought (12)
Angela												
Brody												
Charlene						X	X					X
Chase												
Denise						X	X					
Dominic												
Emily						X	X					
Jerry												X
Jessica												X
Jimmy						X	X					
Jonathan												
Juan		X				X	X					
Lauren												
Marco												X
Marcy												X
Michael						X						
Monica						X	X					
Natalie												X
Vincent												X

Figure 3.5: Sample data—mathematics assessment illustrated in figure 3.4.

Several students also had difficulty with the last problem. A different approach could be taken to respond to this type of problem. Because the data show us that students know the steps necessary to arrive at a correct response but were unable to do so, the issue is in their ability to understand the problem and apply the necessary reasoning to find an acceptable solution. One response could include a class discussion of the problem where students who were successful identify the approaches used and walk through their responses. Another option would be to have students partner with others who were successful so they engage in a fruitful discussion of the problem leading to identifying an accurate solution.

Test items that require students to apply their knowledge and skills and demonstrate understanding are key in gaining confidence that students not only have the skill but can logically apply it. This type of item should be used regularly on all assessments to engage students in tasks that require a deeper, higher level of application. Real-world problems also help students see the connection between the concepts being learned and their importance beyond the classroom.

The collection and analysis of data on traditional assessments require a detailed look at student performance on each concept. A percentage correct or letter grade don't provide an adequate amount of information, and they cannot define and implement a response. There is no one way or one tool to analyze results. Whether using a gradebook, an Excel spreadsheet, a printed grid of student names, or another format of choice, if the data are visual and actionable, student performance will be affected. Color-coding, shading, and labeling data help us to visualize patterns and take action on concerns. As a team, determine the type of visualization that works best for collaborative work. Individually determine the visualizations that make meaning for you.

Rubrics as a Source of Data

The analytical rubric is an excellent source of information on student performance. An analytical rubric is one that first lists the criteria important to successfully completing the product, performance, or standard, and then supplies descriptors of quality at each level of the rubric. Figure 3.6 (page 52) shows the format of the analytical rubric.

A rubric could be generic in nature, which means it can be used multiple times on tasks that are regularly repeated. Figure 3.7 (page 53) is an example of a generic rubric filled out. It provides descriptors of quality that define levels of performance when solving a task. Students receive a score for all criteria on the rubric, so they know their level of performance for each criterion. The rubric also can be considered a feedback tool because it provides students not only with information on their current performance but descriptors associated with the next levels.

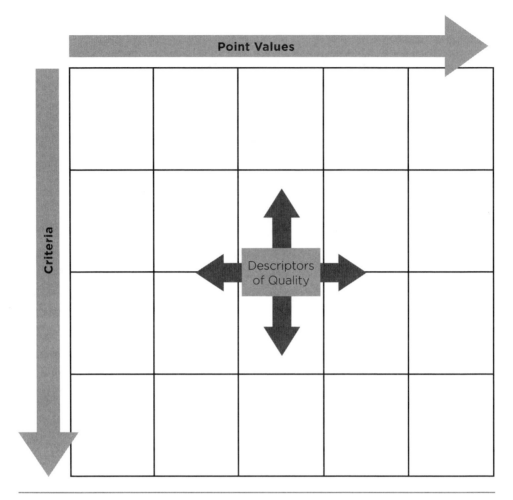

Figure 3.6: Analytical rubric format.

The rubric allows students to locate and identify the highest level of quality. As a result, they can tailor their performance to reach it. The rubric allows teachers to score students by locating the descriptor that most closely reflects student performance. This is repeated for each criterion.

If the intention is to use the rubric collaboratively to encourage inter-rater reliability, consider scoring papers together until a common understanding is developed. Increased inter-rater reliability assists in comparable, quantitative data. Scoring is a matching game; the assessment to the rubric. When teachers share a common understanding of the descriptors, reliability will result.

Criteria	1	2	3	4
Method of Solution (Process)	Solution not attempted or not illustrated	Solution attempted but lacks mathematical sense	Solution illustrated, understandable, and sensible	Solution illustrated, understandable, sensible, and efficient
Solution	Solution not attempted	Solution incorrect or incomplete	Solution correct and complete	Solution correct, complete, and clearly labeled
Demonstration of Understanding	Explanations of solutions show that student does not understand concepts within the task	Explanations of solutions show that student might understand the concepts within the task	Explanations of solutions clearly show that student understands concepts within the task	Explanations of solutions clearly show that student understands concepts within the task and can relate to previous learning
Answer	No clear answer given	Answer apparent but inaccurate	Answer accurate	Answer correct and accurately labeled
Organization	Attempt at organization not apparent	Organization difficult to follow or understand	Well organized, easy to follow and understand	Well organized, easy to follow, easy to understand, clear formation of letters and numbers

Source: Adapted from Burke & Depka, 2011, p. 80.

Figure 3.7: Generic rubric for completing a task.

Gathering and reporting data for a rubric can be a bit more detailed. To best understand and evaluate student performance, a record of the assigned score for each criterion is valuable. Placing the one, two, three, or four on the data sheet highlights exactly how each student performed. Color-coding is also helpful. Each performance level is assigned a color. For example, a score of one is red, two is yellow, three is green, and four is blue. It isn't necessary to use both scores and color-coding, but each can serve a different purpose. The numbers can be manipulated to present a sum or average. Color-coding contributes to a visual that assists in making meaning of the data.

Figure 3.8 illustrates the results of implementing a task from the task solution rubric. Notice that the rubric criteria are listed across the top, and each student receives a score for all criteria.

Student Name	Method of Solution	Solution	Demonstration of Understanding	Answer	Organization	Total Score
Angela	3	3	3	3	2	14
Brody	3	3	4	4	2	16
Charlene	3	4	4	4	3	18
Chase	4	4	3	3	3	17
Denise	4	4	3	3	3	17
Dominic	3	4	3	3	3	16
Emily	3	3	4	4	4	18
Jerry	4	3	4	4	4	19
Jessica	4	4	2	3	2	15
Jimmy	3	3	2	3	2	13
Jonathan	3	3	4	4	3	17
Juan	3	4	4	4	3	18
Lauren	3	4	4	4	4	19
Marco	3	4	3	3	2	15
Marcy	4	3	2	3	2	14
Michael	4	3	2	3	1	13
Monica	3	4	2	3	1	13
Natalie	4	3	2	3	1	13
Vincent	3	4	4	4	2	17
Average	3.37	3.53	3.11	3.42	2.47	15.89

Figure 3.8: Generic rubric results for completing a task.

The last row of the rubric shares the average score for each criterion, making analysis easier when comparing student performance in each area. The last column of the rubric includes the sum of student scores for comparative purposes. On this rubric, a perfect score is twenty.

In figure 3.8, notice there is a dark shading to highlight all ones listed on the data sheet. Twos are shaded a bit lighter than the ones. Threes and fours typically don't require a response to the data but are beneficial in evaluating how well the student is able to perform on the assigned task.

Now that the data are organized, we evaluate and determine what, if any, response is required. The shading highlights two areas requiring a response. The first criterion in need of support is that of organization. Ten students received a one or two as a score, and the average score was by far the lowest among the criteria. Only three students received a four, indicating there is room for improvement by nearly the entire class.

Now what? Address the situation with the class. Relay the importance of organizing thoughts when completing a task so they can be followed and understood by the student and teacher alike. Organization can be a supporting factor in determining an accurate solution. Consider suggesting or providing a graphic organizer that students can use when completing a task. Share student work exhibiting high-quality examples of organization. Prior to assigning a new task, remind students about the value of organization and provide tools and examples to inspire thought.

The column labeled Demonstration of Understanding pinpoints another area of some challenge. If we revisit the rubric, it is clear that the category centers on the explanation of a solution. Sharing of quality exemplars is helpful in this situation and can be used for all rubric criteria. Meet briefly with the six students who struggled in this area. Point out methods of improvement. Remind them of the rubric descriptors associated with higher scores. Perhaps ask them to rewrite their solution, share it with a buddy for feedback, make any desired changes, and submit it to the teacher.

When a generic rubric is used with students throughout the year, they internalize the highest level of quality. Repeated use supports acceptable results and increases the probability of a clear and accurate demonstration of understanding. As the year progresses, responding to the rubric data requires less time because students have had ample practice using the tool. The class has engaged in conversations about quality performance throughout the year. At this point, a response is likely limited to very few students who might struggle with the content yet are familiar with the process to share the results.

Consider, for example, a rubric to evaluate quality writing. When used repeatedly, the students have an increased understanding of the definition and exemplification of quality. As the content or topic of the writing changes, struggles might occur, not due to the process but due to the topic. This distinction will help identify a response that addresses the cause of the struggle. Figure 3.9 (page 56) provides an example of a writing rubric.

Writing Criteria		1	2	3	4
Idea Development	Topic Clarity	Topic is unclear.	Writer strays from topic.	Topic is focused.	Examples and details bring the topic to life.
	Key Ideas	Key ideas do not exist or are difficult to identify.	Additional key ideas or details are needed.	Key ideas and details are clearly expressed.	Clearly expressed details and key ideas enhance theme or story line.
Organization	Structure	Composition lacks structure.	Composition is loosely structured.	Composition is appropriately structured or formatted.	Structure assists in supporting the story.
	Order	Composition lacks logical order.	Order is scattered, difficult to follow.	Order is logical.	Order is logical and effective.
	Introduction Conclusion	Introduction and conclusion are weak.	Introduction or conclusion is weak.	Introduction and conclusion are effective.	Introduction is strong, and conclusion is satisfying.
	Topic Sentence	Composition lacks topic sentences.	Attempt was made to incorporate topic sentences.	Composition has clear topic sentences.	Composition has effective topic sentences.
	Transitions	Composition lacks transitions.	Some transitions are used.	Transitions are used appropriately.	Transitions within and between paragraphs create a smooth flow.
Word Choice	Word Choice	Word choice is vague and confusing.	Word choice is limited or simplistic.	Word choice is clear and functional.	Word choice is precise, detailed, and interesting.

Writing Criteria		1	2	3	4
Voice	Voice	Connection to the audience is missing.	Tone is present but not appropriate for purpose.	Tone fits topic, purpose, and audience.	Tone fits topic, purpose, and audience; writer's personality is apparent.
Fluency	Sentence Variety	Composition has simple, monotonous sentences.	Composition has mostly simple sentences.	Composition has mostly varied sentences.	Sentences vary in structure and length.
	Incomplete Sentences	Fragments and run-ons prevent understanding.	Fragments and run-ons interfere with understanding.	There are few fragments or run-ons, and they do not interfere with understanding.	Composition has well-crafted sentences.
Conventions	Mechanics	Errors interfere with the reader's ability to understand.	Errors are distracting but do not interfere with understanding.	Errors are infrequent and do not interfere with understanding.	Errors are unnoticeable.

Figure 3.9: Writing rubric.

The data that can be collected and reported from this rubric are detailed and actionable. Figure 3.10 (page 58) provides sample data designed according to the rubric criteria. The format should look familiar. It is identical to other reports previously pictured. The darker shading indicates broad categories, then the categories are narrowed. It is helpful to review the detailed data for each portion. For example, the Idea Development category is divided into topic clarity and key ideas. Having data for each individual item provides information regarding students' strengths and challenges. The specificity of the data provides an excellent source of information with which action can be planned. Review the data. What next steps would you suggest? Whenever teachers can group the categories within a rubric into larger categories, but analyze them more discretely with further defined categories, this organization helps students see the connections among the criteria, and helps teachers organize and group data.

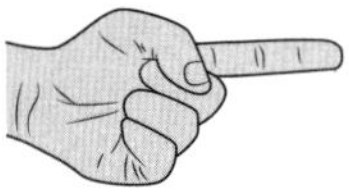	Idea Development		Organization					Word Choice	Voice	Fluency		Conventions
	Topic Clarity	Key Ideas	Structure	Order	Introduction Conclusion	Topic Sentence	Transitions	Word Choice	Voice	Sentence Variety	Incomplete Sentences	Mechanics
Angela												�©
Brody			▒									▒
Charlene												▒
Chase												▒
Denise												▒
Dominic			▒									▒
Emily												▒
Jerry												▒
Jessica												▒
Jimmy						▒						▒
Jonathan												▒
Juan												
Lauren												▒
Marco						▒						▒
Marcy						▒						▒
Michael						▒						▒
Monica						▒						▒
Natalie						▒						▒
Vincent												▒

Figure 3.10: Sample writing rubric data.

Attitudinal Data

Attitude affects student performance. How students behave, understand, and feel influences the strengths and challenges that they display. It is probable that responding to attitudinal data will be noticed in the quality of academic results.

Students are a valuable source of information. They can help us better understand how strategies help their performance. Students can give input on classroom procedures that impact their learning. Factors that are in control of the teacher but not associated with teaching can help students achieve higher degrees of success, or not (Texas Accountability Intervention System, 2012). Let's consider some specific examples.

The comfort level a student has associated with a subject or performance could present challenges to understanding. Apprehension, even fear, can limit student success. In order to respond to unproductive attitudes, however, we first need to recognize that they exist.

Consider conversations with students as a valuable way to get to know students on a deeper level. How do they feel, think, and understand about the subjects you teach? When talking with individuals, we learn about and understand them in ways we are unable to in large-group settings. Practicality can be an issue. Teachers are certainly outnumbered in the classroom, yet on a daily basis the opportunity presents itself to observe and converse with students in the classroom. To whom do we talk regularly? Do we talk to all students individually at least weekly? Keeping track of the data in a very simple way will assist in ensuring that all students have the opportunity to interact with the teacher, one-on-one. These interactions can support the building of relationships. They establish a comfort level with students and help students realize that the teacher is approachable. Students find satisfaction in knowing that the teacher cares enough to check in with them as students and as people on at least a weekly basis. In my own classroom, I realized that I spoke very little to the compliant children who were on task and typically successful. It was not that I purposely ignored them; I truly didn't realize how little attention I was giving them. Attention was paid mostly to those students who presented a challenge.

Consider a simple method to keep track of the times that you speak with individuals in the classroom. Figure 3.11 (page 60) is an example. The data can be gathered using a sheet of paper and a clipboard, or a technological device that provides the ability to access Excel, Word, a gradebook, or any other tool of choice (such as Google Analytics or Twitter Analytics). Note that the format of the data collection tool doesn't need to change. Student names are on the left, and whatever is being evaluated lies across the top. Using the same format repeatedly helps for consistency in reporting especially when data are shared among collaborative teams.

Whom did I talk to this week?

Shade or place an *X* in the box that indicates the day of the week you spoke to the student.

Student Name	Monday	Tuesday	Wednesday	Thursday	Friday
Angela					
Brody					
Charlene					
Chase					
Denise					
Dominic					
Emily					
Jerry					
Jessica					
Jimmy					
Jonathan					
Juan					
Lauren					
Marco					
Marcy					
Michael					
Monica					
Natalie					
Vincent					

Figure 3.11: Tracking sheet for student interaction.

*Visit **go.SolutionTree.com/assessment** for a reproducible version of this figure.*

Student Perceptions

Surveys are valuable in collecting information about students to better understand their perceptions of the classroom. Survey questions can be identified that will provide guidance about our behaviors. Student response data can give us advice. Survey results will report our strengths and opportunities for improvement. Connect the questions asked to aspects that we deem important to student success in our classrooms.

Consider the teacher behaviors that impact student understanding. What beliefs associated with their teacher are important to students' ability to learn and grow? List those that are important in your classroom and ask students how they feel. Figure 3.12 shares an example of a student perceptions survey. The teacher identifies the statements that are reflective of the key points he or she determined to be associated with student success in the classroom.

	Never	Sometimes	Usually	Always
1. I can ask questions when I need to.				
2. I trust my teacher.				
3. My teacher cares about my success.				
4. My teacher teaches in ways that I understand.				
5. My teacher tells me what I do well.				
6. My teacher tells me how to improve.				
7. I can get extra help from my teacher when I need it.				
8. Sometimes I have choices in my assignments, so I can choose the best way to show what I know.				
9. My teacher knows my strengths.				
10. My teacher knows what I find difficult.				

Figure 3.12: Student perceptions survey statements.

*Visit **go.SolutionTree.com/assessment** for a reproducible version of this figure.*

The survey itself includes a scale so that students can evaluate how strongly they feel about any given statement. A yes or no response provides limited information. Too broad a scale can be confusing. Keep it simple, yet meaningful.

Immediately before giving the surveys to the students, provide some background information. Let them know why you are giving the survey and what you will do with the information. The introduction could go something like the following.

> Students, I value your opinions and want to gather some informa-tion from you. I am giving you ten statements about things that I do or don't do that are important to your success in school. I need to know honestly what you think. I plan to use the results of the survey to adjust what I do to better meet your needs. Please respond to each question by placing a mark under the description that you feel best represents your feelings.

Figure 3.13 uses a four-point scale including the choices *never, sometimes, usually,* and *always*. It also includes a set of data that could potentially be an actual response. The numbers in the chart represent the number of students who responded in that category on the survey. Each statement received twenty-seven responses, which reflects the number of students completing the survey.

	Never	Sometimes	Usually	Always
1. I can ask questions when I need to.	12	5	5	5
2. I trust my teacher.	0	3	20	4
3. My teacher cares about my success.	2	5	5	15
4. My teacher teaches in ways that I understand.	5	5	10	7
5. My teacher tells me what I do well.	0	0	22	5
6. My teacher tells me how to improve.	0	0	15	12
7. I can get extra help from my teacher when I need it.	0	0	24	3
8. Sometimes I have choices in my assignments, so I can choose the best way to show what I know.	15	5	7	0
9. My teacher knows my strengths.	0	5	22	0
10. My teacher knows what I find difficult.	0	0	17	10

Figure 3.13: Student perceptions survey and response data.

A good rule to follow is this: only implement a survey when the intention is to respond to the results. The goal with this type of survey is to take it at face value. Results can be perfectly supportive and validating. They can also provide valuable feedback. The results are what they are. It is what we do about them that is important. If on occasion you don't like what you see, don't take it personally; instead, take action. Data are a source of information to which we can respond and grow. Whether we agree with the student perceptions or not, we can develop appropriate responses, implement them, and gather new data after the responses have had time to effect a change in student attitude and in the classroom.

The results listed in figure 3.13 provide information to be proud of yet also include data that indicate action is needed. The results indicate that the students are quite positive about the actions that are the subject of most statements. There is indication that a response is necessary for statements one and eight, and potentially consideration should be given to statement four. The results are cause for reflection.

In response to statement one, I ask myself, "In what ways do I prevent students from asking questions?" I might think about things that I say or do consistently to have students respond this way. Do I provide time for questions throughout the lesson? Am I repeatedly saying, "Hold that thought, we'll get to it," and then sometimes we never do? Do my students understand that questions should be focused on the topic at hand to prevent questions that are distracting rather than meaningful? Is there time prior to or after lessons during which students can get their questions addressed?

The results for statement eight indicate that most students see few opportunities to have assignment options, which has a potential impact on their ability to demonstrate their knowledge and skills with a greater rate of success. How can student choice be increased within assignments and assessments? Do students understand when choice is possible and appropriate? When considering increasing choice, we need to ensure that the options provided will measure the same learning outcomes. We evaluate when choice is possible, and we can work to increase it as appropriate.

Some students, as the results of statement four indicate, feel that they don't understand concepts due to the way they are taught. Evaluating the impact of the strategies used is beneficial to students. The process of reflecting on instructional methods is benefitted greatly when student feedback is incorporated into the reflection. Consider talking to students about the instructional strategies and methods. For example, after using focus questions to inspire group discussion and grow understanding of a topic, ask students what was effective in that approach and what, if anything, was not. Seek input from students on classroom practices that have the greatest impact on their learning.

After taking a survey, it is natural to want to know the results. Share the results with students. Explain how you plan to respond to areas that require attention. This indicates that you are serious about the results and find their feedback meaningful. In the case of the results listed in figure 3.13 (page 62), a conversation may be similar to the following.

> Students, I looked at the results of the survey you responded to yesterday and am thankful for all the information I received from you. I found the results to be quite positive for most of the statements. There are three that caused me to consider some change to current practices. It seems that I don't always give you the opportunity to ask questions when you need to. I will pay closer attention to this. I do want questions to focus on what we are discussing at the time, yet we will find the appropriate time to answer other questions as well. (You might want to share ideas or get input about the topic.)
>
> I also saw that perhaps more choice within assignments or assessments is desirable. That is something that I will definitely consider incorporating more often as possible. (Get input if desired.)
>
> When I teach the class, I use methods and strategies that will help you learn. Because of the survey results, I will be occasionally asking for input on what helps you learn best. If you evaluate the things that we do in the classroom that are most helpful to your learning, we can concentrate on approaches that best meet everyone's needs. (Give an example. Ask for input.)
>
> In a few months, I will be asking you to take the same survey so I can see how opinions vary. Do you have any questions or reactions to what I've said?

During this brief discussion, it would be helpful to have the survey results visible to the students. It is also important to take care that the language used while sharing doesn't appear to blame anyone, including yourself, for the results. There is no blame, only data. We reflect and respond in ways that we feel appropriate.

Attitudinal factors can influence student success. There is importance in skill development, yet a focus on communication, collaboration, growth mindsets, and attitudes that support learning will support long-term learning and success. Skill development in areas including self-management and self-direction will support students' ability to achieve and grow (Zeide, 2016).

Student reflection and self-analysis are powerful. If students are able to recognize and evaluate their strengths and challenge areas, they are more likely to seek improvement when given appropriate support, time, and encouragement. Consider giving a survey in which a student reflects on his or her own traits and dispositions. The results can be compiled for the class if there is a desire to evaluate the status of the class as a whole. To impact change, it is crucial that the student reflects on his or her responses. Encourage a conversation between the student and an adult during which the student can share his or her responses and begin to analyze results and create a plan for growth.

Consider the following survey taken from *Raising the Rigor* (Depka, 2017, pp. 78–79; see figure 3.14).

Category	Please respond to each statement by marking your level of agreement: Strongly Disagree (SD), Disagree (D), Agree (A), or Strongly Agree (SA)	SD	D	A	SA
Collaboration	1. I am comfortable working with most other students.				
	2. I appreciate the opportunity to work with other students in the classroom.				
	3. I feel that I make quality contributions when I work in a group.				
Communication	4. It is easy for me to put my ideas into words.				
	5. When I tell others an idea I have, they understand my idea.				
	6. I am comfortable speaking in front of groups.				
Listening	7. I am told by others that I am a good listener.				
	8. When someone is finished speaking, I am aware of their key points.				
Judgment	9. In most situations I know the best approach to take.				
	10. I weigh options before making a decision.				
Leadership	11. I often find myself coordinating group activities.				
	12. I am frequently asked to lead a group or activity.				

Figure 3.14: College and career readiness—traits and dispositions survey.

continued ➤

Category	Please respond to each statement by marking your level of agreement: Strongly Disagree (SD), Disagree (D), Agree (A), or Strongly Agree (SA)	SD	D	A	SA
Perseverance	13. I like tasks that challenge me.				
	14. I work to find answers even if it is not easy for me.				
Innovation and Creativity	15. I like to create things.				
	16. I often find new ways to do ordinary tasks.				
	17. I invent new games or new ways to play existing games.				
Initiative and Responsibility	18. I usually know what others expect of me.				
	19. Others rely on me to get the job done.				
	20.Others see me as a responsible person.				
	21. I take responsibility for my actions.				

Source: Depka, 2017, pp. 78–79.

After completing the survey, students can be provided with a set of reflective questions to discuss with peers. What personal strengths did you identify on the survey? Which areas would you like to grow in? What will you do to strengthen those areas? Students might also be asked to write a brief statement about their areas of strength, areas that have room for growth, and how students will work to support areas they find more challenging.

A good rule to follow is this: only survey when you, the students, or both will use the results to grow and improve. Spend time processing the survey results with students. Explain how you plan to respond to areas that require attention. Expect students to reflect on and respond to evaluating their own traits and dispositions.

Data can be used successfully on a day-to-day basis to shift instruction and change instructional practices based on student reaction and need. The inclusion of behavioral and attitudinal data provides a rounded picture of students. Consider including factors that influence academic performance like student behavior and absence rate. If it is possible to be proactive and prevent missing classroom activities, the impact will positively influence student performance (Singley & Lam, 2005).

Linking Data to Action

The data review is an ongoing and automatic part of the assessment process. Looking at data in small groups encourages different perspectives and is more likely to yield accurate interpretations. Groups are more likely to pay attention to relevant information. This is not to say that individual analysis is not effective. It is necessary and conducted on a day-to-day basis in classrooms. It does indicate that when possible, analyzing group data with colleagues can provide a variety of viewpoints that possibly would not be considered with a single person analysis (Means, Chen, DeBarger, & Padilla, 2011).

When we hear the words *respond to data*, we may be thinking of assessment results, yet collecting, evaluating, and responding to attitudinal data can help to create stronger classroom practices and strengthen bonds with students. Students responding to their own data establishes a potential pattern of reflecting, identifying challenges, and implementing plans to grow. The process helps students realize that they are very much in control of their future and their ability to experience heightened success. Students share the responsibility for not only the academics, but those dispositions that impact achievement.

These practices encourage life skills that support a rewarding future. Responding to academic data is clearly important to increase understanding and promote success. Responding to perceptions data supports practices and attitudes that impact lives.

To turn data into action, consider the following questions.

- How does the data display impact data analysis? What display methods do you recommend?

- What attitudinal questions do you feel crucial to ask students in your classroom?

- How are student reflection opportunities incorporated in your classroom? Or how will you incorporate them?

CHAPTER 4

Responding to Data: Considerations, Practices, and Procedures

There are many ways to represent data. The key is to make it informative. How we assess, teach, and collect data is part, but not all, of the process. How we respond to data ensures that we give thought not only to students' strengths and challenges but also to what, if anything, we will do about them.

Data can include words, numbers, and observations that are systematically collected with the intention of acting on the results. We collect the data that are appropriate to our purpose, analyze them, determine priorities, and develop strategies to respond to the results (Boudett, City, & Murnane, 2013; van Barneveld, 2008).

Knowing when to respond, creating a systematic and duplicatable approach, and finding time are important considerations when responding to data. To make a response to data possible, we need to be realistic. If everything that is taught during a school year requires a response, we would likely never get through the standards and content crucial to the subject matter. If we are to be realistic, then, we also need to be selective on what requires a response, what we can postpone, and what we can ignore. After each assessment, a systematic and duplicatable approach makes a response possible. However, time is always a factor when we look to respond to student needs. Time is a limited resource so how we make use of it is crucial. There is likely not a perfect way, but there are a variety of possible methods to find time. These areas will be further explored in the pages that follow.

Knowing When to Respond

Sometimes students make a mistake, and sometimes they *misunderstand*. Knowing when to respond is the key. As a reminder, we have already established that frequent assessment results identify misunderstandings before they grow out of proportion. Brief ongoing assessments can identify and clear up misconceptions.

Consider a mathematics assessment in which students are to add two-digit numbers. As part of the assessment, students will demonstrate their skills by solving some equations. A student, who is able to respond correctly to four problems and then makes a mistake, is very likely to know the process. A response is not necessary. The student simply made a mistake. However, if a student consistently displays errors as in figure 4.1, the errors constitute a misunderstanding. A response is necessary.

$\begin{array}{r} 26 \\ +\,48 \\ \hline 64 \end{array}$	$\begin{array}{r} 34 \\ +\,66 \\ \hline 90 \end{array}$	$\begin{array}{r} 59 \\ +\,19 \\ \hline 68 \end{array}$	$\begin{array}{r} 14 \\ +\,19 \\ \hline 23 \end{array}$

Figure 4.1: Sample student errors requiring a response.

The error is repeated and identical. The student is not recognizing that, when adding the ones column, the result is greater than ten. With the regrouping, one ten needs to be added to the digits in the tens column. In each case, the student failed to recognize that each answer is ten greater than the answer given. The sums actually are 74, 100, 78, and 33.

This could be a simple error in procedure. It could also be a misunderstanding of quantity or place value. The procedural error would call for additional explanation, practice, and retesting. If the concept of quantity is confusing, the student will need to engage in activities to understand number size and place value.

During a review of data and error analysis, consider the difference between a mistake and a misunderstanding. Attention can be called to a mistake, and the student can correct it with little or no input from anyone. A misunderstanding reflects a repeated error, one that students are likely unaware they are making because they believe it is the correct way to complete a process or answer a question. If a student forgets to capitalize a single proper noun in a piece of writing, he or she made a mistake. If, however, no proper nouns are capitalized, that reflects a lack of understanding. Students are likely to repeat misunderstandings as time goes on. Students aren't aware that a mistake is being made. They could, in fact, believe that they are correct in their understanding of whatever knowledge and skills they are demonstrating.

A review of the standard will clarify the crucial nature of its content. This will also inform us as to whether an immediate response is essential. An immediate clarification of a misunderstanding will cause it not to become learned. If students simply need additional practice to improve, it may not need to be immediate. A response is needed when the correct demonstration of understanding is important beyond the lesson, it relates to other subject areas, and it is crucial over time and impacts skills important outside of school. Figure 4.2 illustrates essential considerations when determining whether a response to data is necessary.

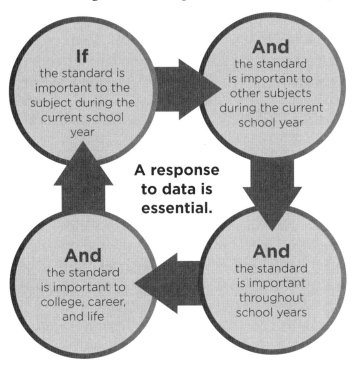

Figure 4.2: Guidelines for determining response to data.

Some standards are taught throughout the year. At the beginning stages of learning, the student might not demonstrate proficiency. If through repeated practice it is likely that the student will perform as required, give time. It is difficult to define learning using time as a key factor. Those standards that continue to develop throughout the year provide the time that some need in order to be successful. It is also difficult to define learning by the number of lessons it will take to help a student reach appropriate levels of understanding. However, it is crucial to identify when the students have completed the learning associated with a standard and the teacher will not need to address it again during the school year. There is a sense of urgency when the student is struggling on concepts that have been developing throughout the year, and time is now at an end. Feedback given throughout the year supports student understanding. Engaging lessons and practice opportunities will assist in preventing a student from progressing too slowly.

Continue to carefully monitor those who struggle, and provide the appropriate amount of challenge and support to help them thrive.

Figure 4.2 illustrates components to consider when determining whether or not a response to data is required. The rich, power standards often contain the basis for future learning and are those that meet all four areas stated in the diagram. A planned curriculum, scope, and sequence assist in determining when to respond to these comprehensive standards that often take a full year to teach. It becomes necessary to know the stages of development associated with the standard at each grade level, throughout each year. The standard can be broken into pieces that are taught throughout the year, each piece building on the next and compiled along the way until all pieces are taught, practiced, and assessed both individually and collectively.

Knowing the stages gives us the background information needed when reviewing and responding to data. Expectations of student performance should match the time line of the scope and sequence. We want students to perform accurately on the concepts and skills that we are confident have been taught and reinforced adequately. If students should be at a point to demonstrate their understanding through their performance, we need to respond if they are unable to do so. Timing is the key. If teachers will continue to teach concepts and students will experience continued learning and have additional time to practice, that is the only response required. Asking students to correct errors is appropriate. Additional practice is likely not needed during early stages.

An example of a deep rich standard is found in figure 4.3. This writing standard details that which a student should be able to do by the end of fourth grade when writing an opinion piece. It meets all of the requirements listed in figure 4.2 and is definitely a powerful standard associated with writing. It is also an example of a standard that is taught throughout the year.

The list of actions that this standard requires is plentiful. All actions are emphasized separately and can be assessed separately during the learning process. Students also need repeated practice on performing all components of the standards. Their level of expertise will grow throughout the year. Care should be taken to assess regularly in order to monitor progress.

When teaching how to introduce a topic, students might first be taught how to state an opinion by providing ample examples and experiences with opinion writing. They are assessed on their ability to state an opinion, and their performance is evaluated. At that point, if any weakness is identified, support is provided. Each component of the standard is added to the next steps in teaching the process. Students are taught about structure and the grouping of ideas. They are

W.4.1: Write opinion pieces on topics or texts, supporting a point of view with reasons and information.

a. **Introduce** a topic or text clearly, **state** an opinion, and **create** an organizational structure in which related ideas are **grouped** to **support** the writer's purpose.

b. **Provide** reasons that are **supported** by facts and details.

c. **Link** opinion and reasons using words and phrases (e.g., *for instance, in order to, in addition*).

d. **Provide** a concluding statement or section **related** to the opinion presented.

What action is the student being asked to do?	What receives the action?
Introduce	Topic or text
State	Opinion
Create	Organizational structure
Group	Related ideas
Support	Writer's purpose
Provide	Reasons
Support	Reasons with facts Reasons with details
Link	Opinions and reasons with words Opinions and reasons with phrases
Provide	Concluding statement
Relate	Concluding statement to opinion

Source for standard: NGA & CCSSO, 2010a.

Figure 4.3: Common Core Writing standard grade 4—write opinion pieces.

also shown how to support the writer's purpose. As each component is taught, it is added to the last. The teaching and assessing of writing is a process of isolation and compilation. Although specific parts of the standard can be taught separately, they are also assessed as a whole.

The isolation and compilation framework in the way lessons are taught leads us to a good understanding of the exact response that is needed. For example, if students are writing a specific statement of opinion and they are struggling, the response is obvious. They may require additional examples, some instruction, peer feedback, and experience in writing an opinion.

As components of the standard are compiled, it is essential to review each component separately in order to adequately evaluate performance. When students are asked to write an opinion piece, their writing should be analyzed based on all criteria listed in the standard. Did they adequately introduce the topic, provide reasons to support their opinion, organize effectively, link ideas, and provide a conclusion? At what level of quality was each performed? Did they meet current expectations, or is a need for support indicated in any of the areas highlighted in the standard?

Student performance should be at or better than the expectation at benchmark points. Common assessments implemented at various benchmark points throughout the year will assist in identifying current strengths, comparing students' performance to that of their classroom peers, and contrasting their performance to that of students at the same grade level. These data will identify needs and support the actions required to improve performance. Provide additional support and practice for students performing below the expected norm. Keep in mind the next steps in the assessed area so that the response is focused on the current need.

Creating a Systematic, Duplicatable Approach to Respond to Data

Responding to data requires us to develop a habit. Establish a routine that becomes an automatic way to do business. Don't waver. Plot the course and move forward. The course may be adjusted along the way, but the end goals remain clear.

The approach we develop doesn't start with responding to data, however; we start at the beginning and assume that a response will be the end point. The approach is a cycle, though, which means that the end point leads to a new beginning, and we start over again. It is continuous.

Consider the start of a unit of study. The cycle we choose to employ starts with the content and standards specific to the learning target and unit. The process we use is duplicated with every unit. Establish a pattern that meets your needs, implement it, and use it repeatedly.

Figure 4.4 shares an approach. Key to the success of the approach depicted is the direct alignment between lesson targets and the tasks and questions developed to assess them. This alignment connects the standard to the demonstration of understanding directly connected to the standard. Student performance on each item provides evidence of student strengths and challenges while giving us the information we need to respond. Chapter 1 provided various examples about this connection. Lessons are designed with student engagement and performance in mind. We consider the teaching approaches and strategies to achieve the best

Steps to Ensure an Effective Response to Assessment Results

Figure 4.4: Circle of student success.

possible outcome. Assignments are identified to engage students in process and content. Assessments are implemented and reviewed. At that point, we enact the systematic approach we use to respond to data. So, what is that approach?

An effective response, then, includes the following action steps.

1. Assign meaningful work.

2. Assess.

3. Analyze the results.

4. Determine the action required.

5. Implement the identified response.

Assign Meaningful Work

This sounds a bit obvious, doesn't it? The goal is to ensure that any assignment given will elicit the best results possible. It is an ineffective use of our time if students are assessed too early in the learning process and are unable to perform adequately. The result is frustrating for student and teacher alike. Timing is critical. There are considerations to keep in mind.

The book *Bringing Homework Into Focus* (Depka, 2015) identifies five aspects of quality assignment design.

1. **Purpose:** Is the purpose of the assignment clear to students? Does the intent of the assignment relate to the targets established? Rarely, if ever, do adults do something for no apparent purpose. We don't see the point. If students are to take an assignment seriously, providing them the purpose will help with the desire to complete it.

2. **Relevance:** Are the students able to understand the connection of the assignment to a larger purpose? For example, has a real-world application been established?

3. **Doability:** Do students have the foundational skills necessary to complete the work?

4. **Quantity:** Is the length of the assignment appropriate? In other words, is it comprehensive enough to ensure a demonstration of understanding without being overburdensome in length? The quantity varies by grade level. Consider multiplying the grade level of the student by ten minutes. This would indicate that a first-grade student would have about ten minutes' worth of work, where a seventh-grade student would have no more than about seventy minutes total.

5. **Design:** Is there a direct connection between the purpose of the lesson and the work assigned? Will successful completion of the assignment indicate if students have the knowledge and skills to proceed?

Capacity is another important consideration when assigning student work or giving an assessment. The capacity to consider is that of the teacher as well as the student. First let's consider the teacher. It takes time to evaluate student performance. If strapped for time and a prompt response to the assessment is not possible, strongly consider other options. Can it be postponed? Is there a way to evaluate student understanding that is time efficient and possible in the current situation?

If students are experiencing a strain on capacity, they will likely not do their best on what is assigned to them. Consider school events that strain energy and assessments given by other teachers. Is there a way to provide balance? The goal is to have students perform to the best of their ability. This will result in fewer gaps in performance. Limited or no response may be required. Considering capacity may be a time-saver when evaluating and responding to results.

Assess

When we assess, the purpose is to evaluate the current status in order to make decisions regarding next steps. The steps are directly related to the demonstration of student understanding on the assessment. Because the assessment results are crucial in determining next steps, they should include the following three characteristics.

1. Be directly related to the standards and content being taught
2. Include the questions necessary to evaluate student foundational skills and background knowledge important to the successful completion of more comprehensive questions
3. Incorporate various levels of rigor into the assessment to evaluate the depth of student understanding

The ultimate goal is to provide students with an opportunity to show what they know on assessments that lead to clear, actionable data.

Analyze the Results

This could sound a bit fuzzy. The word *analyze* is used rather than *correct*. This is intentional. The goal is to not only spot that which is wrong, but to identify patterns that require a response.

What results are being analyzed? *Analyze the results* refers to anything we ask students to do that has the potential of demonstrating their understanding or lack thereof. This might be an in-class or homework assignment, an assessment, or any performance a student is given to complete.

When assigning students work, consider its purpose. If the intention is to build background knowledge prior to new learning, it is important to know if that goal was met. The purpose may have been for students to practice procedures to solidify understanding. Again, it is important to know if the goal was met. The assignment could have been given after students have had ample opportunity to practice and may have been summative in nature. Regardless of the purpose, it is important to know if students achieved the goals set for the assignment.

No matter the purpose of the assignment, feedback on the performance and response to data is necessary in order to help students reach the desired level of success. The purpose of every assignment is to help students apply the knowledge and skills needed in order to reach the targets of the lesson, chapter, or unit of study. Because the assignment is evidence of student understanding, the teacher needs to identify the performance level. If there are gaps or misunderstandings, they can be corrected prior to the next assignment. This type of response requires an immediate analysis of data. Keeping track of how each student performs on assignments, assessments, or any method students use to demonstrate their understanding will provide actionable data and show trends over time. The data that result will not only be valuable but will limit the number of students who require additional support.

Determine the Action Required

A one-to-one (to one-to-one) correspondence can be developed between learning targets, assessment, lesson design, and response to data; these aspects are all connected to each other—the learning target connects to the assessment, which connects to the lesson design, which connects to the response to data. Any time a student is demonstrating their knowledge and skills, the work they are doing is an assessment. This includes classroom assignments and homework assignments of any type. Let's take another look at the standard highlighted in figure 4.3 (page 73). Imagine a lesson based on stating an opinion, and review the information within figure 4.5.

Notice the alignment in figure 4.5. The lesson directly relates to a specific target. The assessment is an application of the target and assigned after completing whole-class and group activities that support learning.

The response is identified prior to knowing if there is a need to respond. It is planned in case it is needed. When the response is planned in advance, it can be worked into the activities of the next class period. In this scenario, the teacher identifies additional time in advance. This immediate response supports student learning and eliminates gaps in understanding before they widen.

The identified lesson response requires students to support the understanding of classmates, and it provides students an additional opportunity to demonstrate their level of proficiency. During the activity, the teacher observes each group and intervenes as necessary to provide support and encourage dialogue. Examples can be shared with the group throughout this portion of the lesson. The response is designed to take a portion of the class period. If the response goes as designed, there will be time to introduce the next step in teaching the standard.

Target Identification	Assessment Following Lesson	Lesson Design	Response
Students will identify and write a quality statement of opinion.	Students will identify statements of opinion from a list provided to them. Students will write a statement of opinion on a topic of their choice.	• Conduct a whole-group presentation defining the purpose of a statement of opinion. • Share examples of quality statements. • Students will work in groups and be given brief opinion pieces to read. They will identify the statement of opinion and critique it. • Findings will be shared with the whole class.	• If students complete the assignment effectively, move on to the next step in the standard. If students experience difficulty, they will share their statement with two peers who will provide feedback. • Students will be given the opportunity to make changes to their work and submit.

Figure 4.5: Connections from target identification to results.

Implement the Identified Response

Consider two purposes to collect and respond to data. The first is frequent, possibly daily, and is conducted with each assignment given to students. In this case, the response is closest to the time the misunderstanding occurs. The good news is that it has not likely had time to become habit and will easily be corrected. The second time we respond to data is with the implementation of each frequent progress check assessment and those summative in nature.

The response to data can be identified during the lesson-design process. As strategies and lessons are developed, ask the question, What will I do differently to reteach the targets if misunderstandings occur related to these concepts? Preplanning will result in a road map. When misunderstandings occur, thought was already given to the response. Considering the response at the time of lesson development is preferable because strategies are already being chosen to use, so instead of identifying one, we think of a few. We don't need to start over after the lesson and spend time in the design process again. The response is identified and will be automatic.

Responding to Frequent Assignments

Often the pattern is to assign students work, correct the work the next day, and go over misunderstandings that surface. This certainly is one approach. Consider another. Provide students with an introductory activity that will engage them in the lesson of the day. During that time, take the opportunity to scan assignments for common errors and misunderstandings. If the majority of the class has some of the same misunderstandings, choose a method to reteach the concept, give the students a limited amount of time to practice, and then add a few practice items to the work already being assigned that day. Limit the practice time and proceed with the work of the day.

If misunderstandings were so plentiful that it is difficult to proceed, perhaps the students didn't have a level of understanding needed to complete the task. In that case, teachers use the strategies previously identified to reteach the learning targets, followed by another opportunity for students to practice. Clearing up confusion immediately will serve to create a strong foundation for future success.

When reviewing assignments, it may become apparent that a few students had difficulty with the assignment. In that case, a minilesson can be presented to the small group of students, followed by a brief practice opportunity and a few practice items added to the work of the day. This immediate response will clarify misconceptions and support the likelihood of enhanced understanding and performance on the follow-up assignment.

Responding to Frequent and Cumulative Assessments

Assessments often evaluate multiple concepts. The pattern for response is the same as with frequent assignments. During the lesson-design process, an alternate strategy or approach to teaching was identified. The assessment data are disaggregated by concept to identify the required response. The response is enacted. With each response, students should be assigned additional practice after reteaching occurs. Their work is reviewed to determine whether performance indicates an acceptable level of understanding.

Students only need to complete work for those concepts they *did not* understand. Choose only that which is necessary to increase understanding. Anything that resulted in an acceptable performance is ignored at this time.

Figure 4.6 reflects the deconstruction of a sixth-grade mathematics standard. The details outlined during the deconstruction process support lesson design. It has been recommended that during lesson planning, a response is identified for the content being taught. This is a time when the teacher is reviewing materials and has each concept fresh in his or her mind. It is the most convenient time to identify an alternate approach to teaching and additional practice opportunities

6.G.1: Solve real-world and mathematical problems involving area, surface area, and volume. **Find** the area of right triangles, other triangles, special quadrilaterals, and polygons by **composing** into rectangles or **decomposing** into triangles and other shapes; **apply** these techniques in the context of **solving** real-world and mathematical problems.		
Action	**Receives Action**	**Additional Information**
Find	• Area	• Right triangles • Other triangles • Special quadrilaterals • Polygons
Compose	• Shapes	• Into rectangles
Decompose	• Shapes	• Into triangles • Into other shapes
Apply	• Techniques	• In context
Solve	• Real-world problems	

Source for standard: NGA & CCSSO, 2010b.

Figure 4.6: Sixth-grade geometry standard.

for students. This saves time and effort later. The response is not delayed. If students have difficulty, the response has been identified and can be implemented immediately. There is no need to go back into resources and find options to support student learning because they have been preidentified.

An example of lesson planning associated with the sixth-grade geometry standard can be found in figure 4.7 (page 82). The portion of the standard being addressed is stated, and the method of assessment is included, followed by the lesson and a response, should students have gaps in understanding. It is a five-day plan with a cumulative assessment given on the last day. However, there is an identified response for each lesson. These responses can be used immediately after the lesson and be relied on after a cumulative assessment.

Consider the following four steps in unit lesson planning.

1. Identify the standard, learning targets, and content of the lessons.

2. Determine how the students will be assessed on each lesson, what quick checks for understanding might be used, and what summative assessments will be identified or created.

3. Determine the strategies and lessons to use when teaching the concepts.

4. Determine how to respond should students falter along the way.

Day 1	Target Identification	• Students will find the area of right triangles.
	Assessment Following Lesson	• Students will complete p. 52, numbers 8-10 and 32 as a formative assessment.
	Lesson Design	• As a class or in small groups discuss, Why find area? • Show the YouTube video 1 demonstrating finding area of right triangle. • Provide a teacher- or student-generated whole-group demonstration of the process. • Implement a small-group activity finding shapes of various right triangles. • For independent work, have students complete p. 53, numbers 1-3 and 25-27.
	Response	• If students need additional support, show video 2. • Prior to additional independent work, have students demonstrate the process using p. 53, numbers 4-5. • Have students independently complete p. 53, numbers 6-7 to demonstrate proficiency.
Day 2	Target Identification	• Students will find the area of other triangles.
	Assessment Following Lesson	• Create and implement an activity as a team-designed quick check.
	Lesson Design	• Discuss, how do these triangles look different from a right triangle? How can we use the formula to find the area? • Show video. Ask student to demonstrate the process for all. • Pair students to find area of various triangles. Check work. • Have students complete the teacher-designed worksheet 5a for independent work.
	Response	• Share area of unusual triangle video. Have student(s) duplicate process. Work with partner to find area of three provided triangles. Independently complete the portion of worksheet 5b that corresponds with needs.
Day 3	Target Identification	• Students will find the area of quadrilaterals.
	Assessment Following Lesson	• Identify and implement a quick check of understanding to be completed as a team.

Day 3	Lesson Design	• Design and implement a minilesson on area of quadrilateral. • Students will work in teams of two to find the area of various quadrilaterals in the classroom. Answers will be compared across teams to check for accuracy. • Students complete independent work—p. 57, numbers 2-6 and 24-28.
	Response	• Share area of quadrilateral video. Have students duplicate process. Work with partner to find area of two provided quadrilaterals. Complete p. 57, numbers 8-10 and 30-32.
	Target Identification	• Students will find the area of polygons.
	Assessment Following Lesson	• Identify and implement a team-designed quick check.
Day 4	Lesson Design	• Class brainstorm session concerning finding the area of a polygon. Provide various polygons and ask, "With the knowledge we already have about area of rectangles and triangles, how might we find the area of the polygons I am sharing with you?" • Students work in teams to find the area of one or two of the shapes discussed. • Students work in pairs to find the area of four shapes provided. • Students complete independent work—p. 63, numbers 4-8, and 12-15.
	Response	• Using test resource, demonstrate breaking the polygon into known shapes. Have students share ideas. Have students find the area of the polygon using the known shapes and adding the areas together. Independent work—p. 63, numbers 1-3 and 16-17.
	Target Identification	• Students will find the area of a combination of triangles, quadrilaterals, and polygons.
	Assessment Following Lesson	• Students complete assessment in figure 4.8 (page 84).
Day 5	Lesson Design	• Students will be given a cumulative assessment.
	Response	• Review data. Refer back to previous methods to reteach part of the lessons. Use the information as a response. Provide alternative independent work if student has already completed the response. • A response is required if student is unable to complete an entire section of the assessment. If sporadic problems are inaccurate, students will make corrections and resubmit.

Figure 4.7: Sample lesson and response development associated with sixth-grade geometry standard.

To clarify, the responses are meant to deal with misunderstandings, not mistakes. Students are capable of correcting mistakes and can be expected to do so independently. Misunderstandings indicate that the student doesn't have the knowledge and skills needed without additional support. The responses to data are designed for these students.

Looking at the assessment in figure 4.8 will help further clarify this point. The assessment is built to evaluate the knowledge and skills of students associated with the lesson plans included in figure 4.7, which is the assessment to implement on day five.

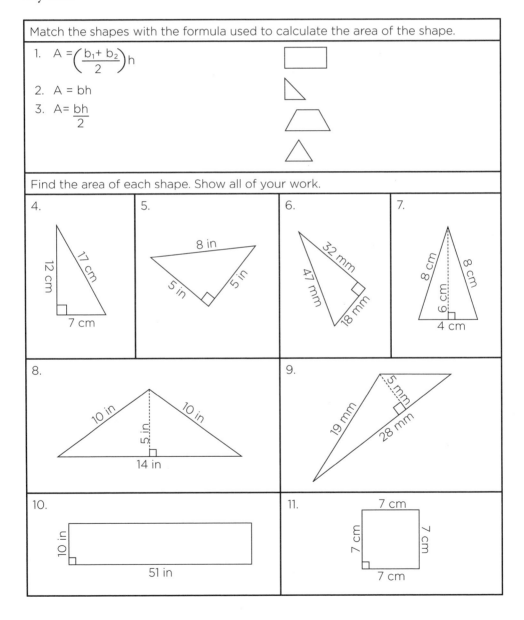

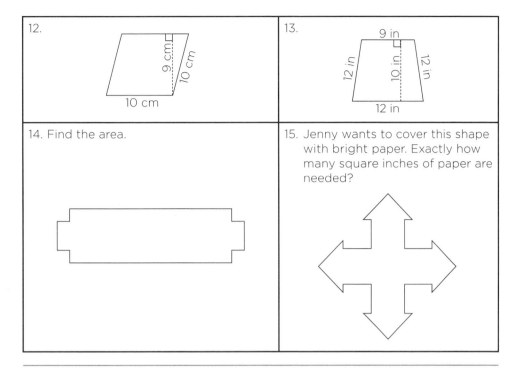

Figure 4.8: Sample assessment based on sixth-grade geometry standard.

Notice that the assessment is organized in the order the lessons were taught, and tasks are grouped according to the shape used. This organization helps in the review of the data. It also helps take students from simple to complex questions to build confidence and remind them of what is needed to solve the problems. The first section of the assessment highlights the formulas. The purpose of this section is to ensure the students know what formula to use with each shape. It reminds them of the formulas to use for the rest of the assessment. If the preference is not to provide the formulas, rather than a matching section, teachers can ask students to write the area formula for each shape.

If students have demonstrated proficiency on portions of the assessment but need support on others, the response should be limited to what the students need help with and should not overburden them with redoing that which they already know. In order to pinpoint the response, review the assessment and the data simultaneously. When data are recorded by question or concept then compared to the knowledge and skills required, the response is definitive. On short single-concept assessments, recording data by question is not necessary, yet it can be informative, especially when the level of difficulty or complexity varies. However, when an assessment has a combination of concepts, whether formative or summative, the data collection helps to determine responses that are required in order to best meet the needs of the students. The visualization of data illustrated in chapter 3 can be useful in this situation as well.

Figure 4.9 provides an example based on the geometry assessment. To easily see the meaning behind the data, compare figures 4.9 and 4.10. Figure 4.10 lists the concepts that students need to know in order to perform well on each grouping of questions from figure 4.8. The shading in figure 4.9 shows which questions had incorrect responses. Two areas surface as needing a response.

Student Name	1	2	3	4	5	6	7	8	9	10	11	12	13	14	15
Angela															
Brody					▓	▓						▓			
Charlene												▓			
Chase												▓			
Denise												▓			
Dominic												▓			
Emily												▓			
Jerry															
Jessica					▓	▓									
Jimmy															
Jonathan															
Juan															
Lauren					▓										
Marco															
Marcy															
Michael					▓										
Monica												▓			
Natalie												▓			
Vincent					▓	▓						▓			

Figure 4.9: Sample student data for geometry assessment.

Questions	If most are incorrect, students are unable to . . .
1–3	Identify the correct formulas to use for each shape.
4	Find the area of a right triangle.
5–6	Find the area of a right triangle with a different orientation.
7–8	Find the area of an equilateral triangle.
9	Find the area of a scalene triangle.
10–11	Find the area of a rectangle.
12	Find the area of a trapezoid.
13	Find the area of a simple unusual shape.
14–15	Find the area of an unusual shape with some complexity.

Figure 4.10: List of concepts in assessment in figure 4.8.

We can see that five students were unable to complete numbers five and six correctly. If we refer to the assessment, we can see in figure 4.10 that those problems asked students to find the area of a right triangle with a different orientation. Because the errors are the result of the orientation of the triangle, the reteaching is related to the error. The teacher can show that the orientation may change, but they should continue to use the sides of the triangle that form the right angle to determine the area. As an example, students can find the area of a triangle with the orientation that they understood. They can then shift their paper to see how the area stays the same regardless of orientation. The teacher can then lead students to understand that regardless of orientation, they are to look for the right angle and use the legs of the triangle to complete the process. Students would then try the problems again. This may be enough guidance. If they are struggling beyond that, we refer back to the lesson plans and follow the plan established for the response on day one as seen in figure 4.7 (page 82). This process is complete only for those concepts deemed essential at this time.

The data also show that nearly half of the class struggled with finding the area of a trapezoid. The response identified for day three can be implemented, tailoring it to the video and tasks that deal specifically with trapezoids. Because of the number of students who had difficulty, an alternative could be engaging the class in an activity dealing with finding the area of a trapezoid. Students can be grouped so there is a combination of those who struggled and those who did not. A real-world problem could be posed which will support the last part of the geometry standard. Figure 4.11 (page 88) is an example. Following the activity, a few independent problems should be assigned to students who struggled to ensure that they now understand.

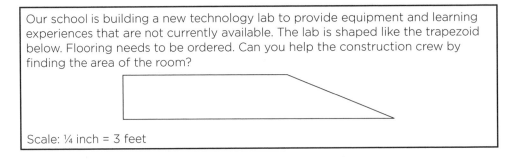

Our school is building a new technology lab to provide equipment and learning experiences that are not currently available. The lab is shaped like the trapezoid below. Flooring needs to be ordered. Can you help the construction crew by finding the area of the room?

Scale: ¼ inch = 3 feet

Figure 4.11: Example of real-world problems—finding the area of a trapezoid.

Because a response was preplanned for students requiring additional support, the follow-up could be automatic. After administering the test and reviewing the data, misunderstandings in any area are matched to the previously identified response and enacted. Figures 4.6 through 4.10 illustrate the connections to and the thought behind each step. It is not necessary to script all of the steps unless desired. However, it is necessary to think through the steps, especially those listed in figure 4.10. This process is easily duplicated and takes limited effort when responses are identified during lesson design.

Finding Time to Respond

In order to respond to student needs, time needs to be available to teachers. Identifying the time available is necessary in order to implement any response to an assessment. Whether the time occurs within or outside of the school day, during class time or outside of the class period, through rearranging schedules or sharing students among teachers, or by any other method, finding time is crucial to a successful response. The sections that follow consider a variety of examples that teachers can use to find time to respond. Because the use of time is different for various types of assessment, we consider daily class time structure, frequent progress checks, common formative assessments, common summative assessments, intensive intervention, and student responsibilities.

Daily Class Time Structure

Time is precious. There is a defined amount of it during the school day that is controlled within the classroom. There is reason to consider classroom procedures along with the use of time in an attempt to limit the amount of time needed to respond to student misunderstandings.

Let's revisit the concept of doability mentioned earlier in this chapter. As a reminder, *doability* refers to the ability of students to complete an assignment.

Prior to giving students a task to complete independently, we want to have a level of confidence that they are ready to complete the task. Readiness guarantees that fewer mistakes will be made, and students are more likely to succeed, requiring less time to respond. If this is the case, evaluating the likelihood of student success prior to giving an assignment is beneficial.

Any assignment is not only practice for students, but also an assessment of their skills and abilities. Responding to a misunderstanding as close to its discovery as possible prevents it from being learned. Unlearning can be more difficult than learning. With that in mind, it is clear that gaining an assurance of students' comfort level with new knowledge is essential prior to assigning independent work.

What can be done to solidify our knowledge that students know and understand at a level appropriate to their ability to engage in independent practice? Consider engaging in formative practices that gather information from students. Table 4.1 (page 90), from *Bringing Homework Into Focus* (Depka, 2015, p. 29), provides some examples.

Key to determining an appropriate timing in assigning a task or assessment is having a great deal of confidence that students are ready. Informal strategies like those in table 4.1 are helpful. Practices exercised in the classroom on a daily basis are crucial to student success. Through observation and other practices, teachers gain a wealth of knowledge about their students. This information informs practices moving forward (Schifter, Natarajan, Ketelhut, & Kirchgessner, 2014). Observation is a powerful tool and a perfect example. Frequently, lessons are designed with an instructional activity, followed by both large- and small-group interactions, followed by independent practice. During small-group work, wandering the room and gathering observational data lead to an understanding of student competency. To gather additional information, students can be assigned a short task to complete which can be corrected and discussed to ensure students are ready to practice independently. At this point, there is ample information to determine whether to proceed with independent work. Ultimately, the goal is to have students experience the greatest possible success during their first experience with the concepts taught. Additional time is less likely to be required, and the class can proceed with the next lesson. Providing time to begin and gain confidence with independent work during the class period will also support successful completion of the work.

This, of course, is the ideal. When all students are successful in assigned tasks, plans can proceed smoothly with no delays or interruptions. We all know that this is not always the case, so when we need time, how can we find it? One way is through lesson structure. If not already available, it is beneficial to consider

Table 4.1: Informal Formative Assessment Strategies

Strategy	Description
Pre-exit slips	Pre-exit slips are distributed and collected within the last ten minutes of class. Questions are asked to determine student readiness. Students might be asked a specific question, the answer to which would determine readiness (for example, a specific type of mathematics problem). An alternative would be a more traditional approach, including a statement, question, and confidence level, such as: (1) Explain the procedure you just learned. (2) What question do you have? (3) On a scale of 1–10, what is your level of confidence with this material?
Whiteboard responses	The teacher asks students to respond to a question or complete a procedure like that which will be expected on the homework. Each student completes his or her response on a mini-whiteboard or sheet of paper. When the appropriate amount of time has passed, students hold up their work so the teacher can evaluate the level of success.
Stoplights	Students are given a stoplight that they keep with them during the class period. Teachers share with students the homework expectations and provide a sample exercise. Students listen to the explanation. A question similar to that of the homework is then posed to the students. The students formulate their responses and then point to the red, yellow, or green lights to illustrate their level of confidence with the answer. Green means, "I'm ready to go!" Yellow means, "I'm not confident I can move on." Red means, "I'm at a standstill. I can't proceed."
Thumbs-up!	Any type of reflection can be used that requires a student to evaluate their level of understanding and communicate that to the teacher. Thumbs-up requires teachers to simply ask students to reflect on their confidence with the content, skills, or procedures. Students indicate a thumbs-up if they are ready to move on. Thumbs-down indicates that more support is needed.
Feedback loops	Students are each given a question to answer or problem to complete based on the work they will be expected to complete. The students are given time to complete the task. In partner groups, the students explain their work to each other, including any procedures or strategies used as well as their answers.
Me-We-You	This strategy requires the teacher to share an example with the class. A similar task is assigned to students in small groups, and then the students are asked to perform a similar task on their own. The teacher evaluates students' confidence level at each step: Me (the teacher)—We (small groups)—You (the student).

Source: Depka, 2015, p. 29.

allotting time within each lesson to work with individuals or small groups of students who need support. An activity designed to collect feedback regarding current understanding of the day's lesson targets is also recommended in order to determine whether students have the basis of understanding necessary to engage in independent practice. Figure 4.12 provides one example of a possible structure.

10 percent of class	The purpose of the introductory activity is twofold. First is to engage students immediately upon entering the classroom or beginning the subject. Secondly, it frees up time for the teacher to work briefly with an individual or small group. Suggestion 1: This activity can be based on the lesson of the prior day's work and remind students of the procedures used in the assignment. Students answer one to two questions based on the assignment from the previous day. Teachers can share answers or students can share them collaboratively. Suggestion 2: Answers to the previous day's work are posted. Students compare their work to the answers to evaluate accuracy. Suggestion 3: A task is posed on relevant content at the beginning of the week, and students engage in the task at the beginning of each class.
30 percent of class	The teacher presents the lesson, engaging students as designated during the lesson-design process.
30 percent of class	Lesson continues with students engaged in group or independent activities to further the targets of the lesson.
10 percent of class	Students are assigned a task to provide feedback on their current proficiency with the content of the day. The teacher uses this information to assess readiness for independent work.
20 percent of class	Students begin independent work. The teacher observes students and answers questions as they arise. If students are not yet ready to complete work independently, the teacher reinforces concepts of the day, possibly having students work together to increase readiness.

Figure 4.12: Structure and use of class time.

Figure 4.12 provides an example of one way of using class time. Time allotments can be tweaked as necessary to adjust to the number of minutes available and the requirements of the subject. Consider the number of minutes available, determine where time can be used to work with small groups or individuals to respond to identified needs, and decide what the rest of the class will be doing during that time. A structural design that allows time to meet with students will save time in the long run because students are more likely to experience success when concerns are addressed as close to immediately as possible.

Structuring time within the class to eliminate misunderstandings and observe students working on new concepts may seem difficult due to time constraints. In the long run, however, this structure indicates that misunderstandings are corrected as soon as they arise.

Frequent Progress Checks

Brief cumulative assessments serve an important purpose. They provide students with the opportunity to demonstrate understanding on a limited number of concepts at a time, combining learning targets associated with previously taught lessons. Students are required to demonstrate formerly practiced skills and understanding on targets associated with past successful performance. If they were not successful when the targets were originally introduced, a response was associated with their misunderstanding in order to support enhanced learning and provide additional practice.

The expectation associated with frequent progress checks is that students will perform well because they have previously experienced success. Realistically, this is not always the case. Combining learning targets into a single assessment can be more difficult for some. Some find it harder to remember and apply procedures formerly learned. Should the data require some response, the amount of time required to respond to needs should be determined. Consider the following questions. (Although these questions are particularly useful for frequent progress checks, they can apply to almost any assessment type.)

- Which students made errors that can be self-corrected without much, if any, input from the teacher?
- Which students appear to misunderstand and need additional instruction to be successful?
- How many learning targets will require time for reteaching and support?
- What responses require teacher and student time?
- What responses require time from the students?
- How much in-class time can be devoted to working with students or groups with misunderstandings compared to how much time is needed?

Following a short assessment, there will be fewer concepts on which a response is necessary. The limited scope also causes students to concentrate on just a few applications or procedures at a time. As a result, the time needed to work with students and eliminate misunderstanding is less. It is possible that it can be worked into the class time already scheduled. The timing is important because the sooner the misunderstanding is cleared up, the more likely students will experience success on the remainder of the unit. The more immediate the reaction to the data, the better it is for students. Because each concept assessed has also been practiced and assessed independently prior to the short cumulative assessment, it is reasonable to think that the success rate will be significant.

It is certainly possible that supporting learning needs will require more time than allotted during a class period. The following are some suggestions to consider in efforts to find supplementary time.

In the self-contained classroom where one teacher is responsible for all academic subjects, consider shaving five minutes off of the time allotted for each subject. An additional twenty to twenty-five minutes will be the result. The time can be placed in the most appropriate location during the school day to support student needs. If possible, the placement can be flexed to immediately follow the subject requiring a response to assessment. For example, if time is to be spent working with students on misunderstandings in mathematics, the time can be placed immediately after mathematics. If English language arts is the area of concentration, the time would be placed after (or before) that class period. Adding time to each subject as needed serves to place the time where it will have the greatest impact on student performance. It will also balance time throughout the year so that the five minutes removed originally to create the block will not result in a continued loss of time for a single subject. The schedule is just a rearrangement of when the time will be used.

If the teacher is able, response sessions can be created following each brief cumulative assessment at a time that is possible. For example, many educators find time prior to and following the school day to meet with students. Because these times are outside of the school day, it is sometimes difficult to make them mandatory for students who require support. However, if parents are involved and supportive, and there are ways to get students to school early or picked up after the sessions, the time is valuable. Often buses drop students off well before the start of the day, so this time may already be available.

Although it is difficult to take students out of different subjects and activities to provide support in that which is deemed essential, it can be considered. Temporarily using time committed to another subject may be an option. Teachers need to come to an agreement, and the time needed should be acceptable so that students can continue to make progress and engage in all subjects. This approach is not one that will be needed on a regular basis if the assessment structure in each classroom follows the recommendations previously stated. The goal is to assess frequently, giving students the opportunity to demonstrate competence daily, followed by a brief assessment to pinpoint misunderstandings before a learning gap becomes a chasm. An immediate response will greatly reduce the need for lengthy intervention. Typically, this need is the result of students who come into a grade level with broad gaps in understanding. These students may need long-term support and are candidates for intensive intervention.

When limited or no responses to student assessment results are required, time for other activities is increased. With that in mind, during unit planning or weekly lesson planning, consider the information in figure 4.13, which provides an option to increase successful completion of student assignments. If within each lesson, a brief assessment is incorporated into the plan and we gain confidence that students are ready to practice the concepts, they are more likely to be successful. Using this method daily will compound the impact when administering cumulative assessments.

1. Identify standards and learning targets to teach.
2. Create or identify a brief assessment to evaluate student understanding of the lesson.
3. Determine the strategies and engaging activities to use to teach the lesson.
4. Identify the method to use for students to practice the day's targets.
The order of events: Share lesson targets with students. Implement planned lesson, including engaging activities. Have students complete the brief assessment. If students are confident as the results of the assessment indicate, assign the practice activity to solidify understanding.

Figure 4.13: Daily lesson-design process.

When responding to brief classroom-driven assessments, identifying the time to respond is tied to the ability and flexibility of the teacher. Consider scheduling time that best meets both the needs of the teacher and the student, with in-class time being the first option considered. When working collaboratively with a team, additional options are available.

Common Formative Assessments

The beauty of common assessments when considering data response is that there are multiple teachers to share the responsibilities associated with the response. Certainly, individual teacher responses continue to be a possibility, but finding alternatives is worthwhile so that efforts aren't duplicated throughout the school. Instead, time is used as efficiently and effectively as possible.

The probability of sharing students when responding to data can be limited if class periods vary and a common time is not available during which students can be shared. However, if a method to share students can be identified, the outcome is worth the effort.

Take a moment to review the deconstruction of the writing standard in figure 4.14, and then look at the data reported in it. The data report the total number of students needing assistance in each class for each portion of the standard.

W.3.2: Write informative/explanatory texts to examine a topic and convey ideas and information clearly. a. Introduce a **topic** and group **related information** together; include **illustrations** when useful to aiding comprehension. b. Develop the **topic** with facts, definitions, and details. c. Use **linking words and phrases** (e.g., *also*, *another*, *and*, *more*, *but*) to connect ideas within categories of information. d. Provide a **concluding statement or section**.		
Verbs or Actions	**Receives action**	**Additional Information**
Introduce	• Topic	
Group	• Related information	
Include	• Illustrations	• When useful
Develop	• Topic	• With facts • With definitions • With details
Use	• Linking words • Phrases	• To connect ideas
Provide	• Concluding statement or section	

Source for standard: NGA & CCSSO, 2010a.

Figure 4.14: Deconstruction of writing standard.

As we look at figure 4.15 (page 96), we can see that eleven students can use support on introduction, ten on conclusion, and thirteen on topic development. It is likely that writing will be taught throughout the year and students will get repeated practice. However, the common assessment is typically designed after students have had some opportunity to practice. Any common assessment should result in a response if the data indicate the need.

In this case, students could be divided into three groups for a defined number of class periods. Students in group one are those who did not have difficulty, group two had difficulty with the introduction or conclusion, and group three had difficulty with topic development. If students had difficulty in all three areas, determine their area of greatest need. The three groups are each assigned to one

Results	Introduction	Grouped Information	Illustrations	Topic Development	Linking Verbs and Phrases	Conclusion
Class 1	6	0	0	4	0	8
Class 2	5	0	0	7	0	1
Class 3	0	0	0	2	0	1
Totals	11	0	0	13	0	10

Figure 4.15: Data collection for writing standard assessment—students struggling.

of the three teachers. Typically, the teacher whose students had the best results in an area would teach that area to students who struggled.

Groups are not of a balanced size. In this example, group one will be much larger but doesn't require reteaching because students were successful on the common assessment in all areas. They can engage in a writing experience that teacher one designs to take them to the next level of expertise. Teacher two can work with introduction and conclusion, providing a lesson and student engagement, perhaps using the common assessment as a starting point and retooling the original to create a quality piece. Similarly, the teacher of group three provides instruction and feedback regarding topic development. Students can enhance their common assessment to apply new learning.

The time allotted should be equivalent to student need and the importance of the standard. Understandably, classes of the same content area or course don't always occur at the same time. In that case, a different tack might be taken. Students who struggled can meet with the teacher when time permits. It helps if all students who struggle in the same area can meet at the same time. The students can be divided among the three teachers according to the content and response required. Although not ideal, meeting prior to school, during lunch, or after the school day is an option. Some schools have a resource time built into the day during which students and teachers can meet for purposes like this.

The time should be focused, organized, and run like an instructional period. The intention is not to have students drop in and work solely on strengthening their assessment. Instruction and new learning are needed. The format used is flexible and is identified because of its benefit to students.

Common Summative Assessments

Common summative assessments are often conducted at the end of a unit of time like a chapter. Timing for the response can be different if the assessment covers standards and content that will not resurface. If success with new learning will not be dependent on the performance on the common assessment, timing is flexible. Data should be collected and organized. Student performance should be analyzed and discussed. Next steps should be identified.

The next steps might be different than when responding to a short-cycle common assessment. Because the assessment was cumulative and summative, a response to student understanding might be placed in the hands of the student. Ample opportunities have been provided leading up to the larger cumulative assessment. Students have had multiple opportunities to show what they know. They have been provided relearning opportunities and have been supported along the way. At this point, consider asking students the questions that follow. (Although these questions are particularly useful for common summative assessment, they can apply to almost any assessment type.)

- How does your performance compare to the targets of the assessment?

- What can you do to improve your performance?

- What help do you need from me?

Often students are given time and support to improve summative results because of the direct connection to receiving a report card grade. The extra time and effort a student puts into their learning will benefit long-term understanding. The purpose of this engagement is not to simply correct errors, but to engage in activities that will instruct and provide increased understanding. After their learning is reinforced, they can demonstrate their knowledge and skills in a method appropriate to the task and connected to concepts the student misunderstood on the assessment.

Collaborative discussions with teaching colleagues can center on other aspects of the assessment. Consider the following questions.

- On what portions of the assessment did most students demonstrate a clear understanding of content and procedures?

- If difficulties were evident, on what content or procedures did students struggle? Were any of the assessment items particularly difficult?

- Why might that be the case?

- Are there certain instructional strategies that worked particularly well?

- Were any resources more helpful than others?

- When teaching the same chapter or unit the next time, what considerations should be made to increase learning?

- What should be repeated due to the rate of success that followed?

- What, if anything, needs to be retaught immediately because the next unit of learning is dependent on current understanding?

A response to a summative cumulative assessment may look different, but it is as important as responding to the results as with formative assessments. The response looks different, yet it has a direct influence on student performance. By the time a summative assessment is given, misunderstandings indicate that, although a student has had previous opportunities to practice and demonstrate understanding, he or she continues to be unsure. As a result, the preceding questions are instrumental in determining why misunderstandings continue to surface and, most importantly, what will change in the future to decrease the potential of a repeat of the same.

Intensive Intervention

A student who is performing well below that of his or her peers requires a different response. This student requires intense, long-term assistance to gain the knowledge and skills equivalent to those already used proficiently by grade-level peers. In this case, the student is likely being monitored within a response to intervention (RTI) system. As Burke and Depka (2011) note:

> RTI is a structure that aligns instruction and systems of assessment, data collection and analysis, and interventions to best meet the academic and behavioral needs of students. It is based on the belief that all students—including English learners, students with disabilities, students who are economically disadvantaged, and students of all ethnic backgrounds—can learn if they are given the proper materials, strategies, and interventions. The goal of RTI is to maximize student achievement through the use of effective instruction strategies while teaching and promoting behaviors that are supportive of the learning environment. (p. 5)

Traditionally, RTI consists of three tiers: Tier 1 represents core instruction, Tier 2 represents supplemental interventions, and Tier 3 represents intensive student supports (Buffum, Mattos, & Malone, 2018).

When a student is performing below grade level (Tier 1), teachers discuss supports for students within and beyond the classroom. If deemed appropriate, the student may be provided classroom instruction (Tier 2) as well as intensive intervention (Tier 3) to decrease learning gaps. The classroom teacher will provide daily supports to the student, but that alone may not be enough. Determining how far behind a student is and catching him or her up to his or her peers is a discussion that involves a team of educators who can support the classroom teacher. For example, if the student is three years behind, a support team is appropriate. Discussion will likely include what strategies, practices, adjustments, and supports need to happen in order to create a time line that will catch the student up to an acceptable grade-level performance. Identifying key learning and creating an accelerated pathway will be crucial to close the gap. Although the responses to data previously discussed in this book will support the growth of this student, more support is needed to eliminate significant gaps. (See *Using Formative Assessment in the RTI Framework* [Burke & Depka, 2011] and *Taking Action* [Buffum et al., 2018] for more about implementing RTI for students performing below grade level.)

Student Responsibilities

The person most essential to the long-term success of any student is the student. As a result, any response should include the student as a key player. The teacher can guide him or her to an experience designed to increase understanding, yet the student needs to engage and commit to the learning process. The response to data is not limited to correcting an incorrect response. That works only when the student has made a mistake and knows how to correct it. If he or she has a misunderstanding, more is required. The misunderstanding is identified and action taken only on the area of confusion. Limiting the reteaching to just the required areas is a time-saver and more palatable to the student.

If the lesson planning recommendation suggested earlier is followed, a method to reteach has already been identified. If not yet identified, a method of reteaching should be established. A minilesson the teacher or another student conducts can work. Using online videos to share a concept or procedure is beneficial if possible with the lesson targets. This can also be a time-saver for the teacher. After receiving additional instruction, the student should be provided a practice opportunity in order to solidify understanding. After the teacher provides feedback, the student can redo his or her original work if the teacher deems necessary.

Depending on the policy for grading and reporting, the student may choose or be asked to redo the work to demonstrate proficiency to replace the grade he or she previously earned.

The student should have an active role in this journey. If appropriate to the grade level, after an assessment the student can evaluate his or her misunderstandings and determine how to best learn the material. The student can also identify how to best demonstrate his or her newfound knowledge. Figure 4.16 can be used with students to assist this process.

Name	Today's Date	Date to Complete Plan
I need to better understand the following:		
I plan to learn more by doing the following:		
I will show that I gained understanding by doing the following:		
Student signature	Teacher signature	

Figure 4.16: Template to gather student responses to assessment results.
*Visit **go.SolutionTree.com/assessment** for a reproducible version of this figure.*

At first glance, it might seem that this would initially be difficult for students, which may be accurate. However, if this is an approach that is intended to become systematic, during the early stages, students will need suggestions on how to access information and gain understanding about content. This knowledge will be transferred to future needs, and students will begin to better understand how to use the resources available to them to access the information they require. This approach doesn't eliminate the need for teacher-led reteaching activities, but it can be used as often as possible to engage students in finding ways to meet their needs. The process engages students in an approach that supports a lifelong skill.

Figure 4.17 provides an example of the completed form. Students should be clear with their method of learning. They also need to have an exact and appropriate way to demonstrate their new understanding. The completion date is an important component. The time allowed for a response should be reasonable, but not lengthy. A quick response is the best for a few reasons. It doesn't place students in a situation where they have multiple responses going on at the same time, and the new learning comes as close to the time of the assessment and initial teaching as possible.

Name	Today's Date	Date to Complete Plan
Dwight	*April 3*	*April 10*
I need to better understand the following: *I am not very clear on how to identify a theme because I'm not sure of what a theme is. Because I didn't know what it is, I couldn't support it with evidence from the text.*		
I plan to learn more by doing the following: *I'm going to find and watch a YouTube video that talks about theme, and I'm going to ask MaryBeth to explain it to me because she really understands it.*		
I will show that I gained understanding by doing the following: *After I know what to do, I will redo the work that confused me on the assessment. I will also ask the teacher if there is anything else I should read to show that I really understand theme and how to support it with evidence.*		
Student signature *Dwight S.*		Teacher signature *Mrs. Doyle*

Figure 4.17: Sample student response to assessment results.

Determining What Data Require a Response

The short answer is yes, yet the response required can be vastly different. A basic but essential response begins whenever students are asked to complete an assignment. If students are asked to perform in any way, feedback provides them an awareness of how their work compares to the expectation. Feedback is directly related to an increase in student performance because an understanding is gained that assists students in recognizing where they are now and what they need to do to arrive at the next level of quality. Feedback is informative. Feedback supports learning.

Let's consider specifically the response to assessment data. Table 4.2 (page 102) provides the type of response indicated for situations that may occur. Analyze the data and consider first if any reteaching is necessary. If not, celebrate accomplishments with students and continue to the next level of learning. If mistakes or misunderstandings occur, identify the essential and enact the desired response to support student learning. With any response, it is important to collect evidence that it has been successful. As a result, students will need to practice and provide evidence that their understanding has risen to a new level and they are able to perform proficiently.

Table 4.2: Situation-Response Possibilities

Situation	Response
Data indicate that all students demonstrate understanding at an acceptable level of proficiency.	Share the outcome with students and celebrate!
Students make occasional mistakes on assessment.	If students made a mistake, they are likely able to self-correct because they understand what they are to do, but they made errors while completing their work. Students review assessment and correct errors.
Students misunderstand as indicated by the inability to complete a section of like concepts on the assessment correctly.	Group students who have the same misunderstanding, and initiate the response identified to clear up the misunderstanding. The response includes instruction, practice, and reassessment.
Large numbers of students misunderstand the same portion on the assessment.	This can indicate that the assessment was given before students had solidified their understanding. Plan a lesson including different strategies that you used to teach the concept originally. Provide students a practice opportunity. Review their work. Implement assessment if performance indicates students are ready.
A single student struggles throughout the assessment.	Identify the essential content. Create a learning path for the student to gain the needed understanding. The path should include new learning, practice, feedback, and assessment. Because the student will be acquiring this new knowledge while continuing with other classwork, the path developed should be succinct and doable, concentrating on that which is essential to his or her ability to succeed in the future.

Linking Data to Action

Class time is precious. There is so much to accomplish in any given school year. Consider the nature of any potential response. Choose to respond to that which is essential for that moment and time and into the future. Involve students in the process as they truly are the key players. Develop systems of response that work for you, in your situation, and with your collaborative team.

To turn data into action, consider the following questions.

- Knowing when to and when not to respond to data is an important consideration. Before beginning a new unit of

study, how do you determine which concepts or procedures
will require a response should students demonstrate a lack of
understanding?

- What is the systematic approach you use or your collaborative
  team uses to ensure that the response to data can be
  automatically implemented in a timely fashion?

- How do you currently find time to respond to student need,
  and what other practices might you consider?

CHAPTER 5

Encouraging Students to Respond to Data

Students have a need for belonging, support, and security in school relationships. They also benefit from feeling they have some control over their school lives. Ownership in school can result from allowing students to take ownership in their learning and explore their ideas. Students need to understand the relevance of the learning tasks they are asked to engage in. We want students to be self-reliant and construct meaning from their learning and their misunderstandings. Students should engage in critical thinking (Stefanou, Perencevich, DiCintio, & Turner, 2004).

Students who are confident in their abilities have an advantage. In order for students to be successful in responding to data, they need to believe that they are capable and that their time and action will result in success. "There is incredible power in students' beliefs about themselves and their own abilities. These beliefs influence confidence, effort, attitudes, and achievement" (Erkens, Schimmer, & Vagle, 2017, p. 118).

When considering data, we often think of teachers' analysis and action. Including students in the process encourages them to understand and react to their personal data. This chapter considers components that support student involvement.

As teachers work with students to respond to their assessment results, they spend worthwhile time providing students with an understanding of data, their value, and their use. Through these efforts, they create a data culture with students, which we explore in the next section.

In the sections that follow, you'll also explore how to best help students understand and use data, be proactive in this understanding to independently record and analyze their progress, and set goals. When students set goals, they understand that they are working to learn but also to reach new levels of attainment and expertise. Through the recommendations and strategies in this chapter, students can take an active role in effectively responding to data.

Building a Data Culture With Students

Building a culture of data with students is not unlike that which we consider with teachers. Essential components include trust, the ability to view and understand, and the knowledge that an action is the intended outcome.

Consider establishing an atmosphere of student trust when it comes to reviewing data. Using data effectively relies on a culture of trust and support. Just as teachers need this when analyzing data with colleagues, students also need to feel that trust is prevalent, and support is present (Lachat & Smith, 2005). In order to be able to view and interpret their own data, students need to know that the analysis is a matter of course. It does not occur because they have performed poorly; they are not "stupid." They simply might need to gain some deeper understandings in order to perform at an increased level of success. A data review doesn't happen only when the student is unsuccessful. It should be a systematic response following any performance. The data analysis might show the students that their performance was exactly on target.

Students and teachers alike benefit from knowing that data are what they are. There should be no blame or admonishment. The crucial reason to review data is to determine the action associated with information gleaned from the data. To embed data analysis by students into classroom practices, three things are required: time, training, and action. Consider the following conversation at the onset of implementing a system of data analysis and use by students.

Teacher: Students, I am returning to you the assessment you took yesterday. In our classroom when you take an assessment, I review the data for the class and determine what I need to do as a result. Sometimes I may need to determine some alternative strategies to use to reteach a concept. At times, I might create short-term groups of students where we will respond to some of the data I reviewed on the assessment. Sometimes we may celebrate our success and move on. After every assessment, I will involve you in the process. The ability to review our own performance and analyze our strengths and weaknesses is a skill that is important not only in our class, but in life. Each of you will take an active role in looking at your results, determining strengths, and identifying areas of confusion if they exist. After reviewing your results, I will ask that you identify the next steps you feel are necessary to solidify your understanding. To help you in this process, you will receive the corrected assessment, and I will provide some feedback on the assessment for you to use during your analysis.

I want you to understand that your performance is personal. Any mistakes that are made can be corrected. Any misunderstandings can be cleared up. What you will see when reviewing your results may indicate a perfect performance. That would be great! If it doesn't, however, it simply means that a bit more learning is necessary in order to reach a higher level of performance. You will look to see what caused the error and take an active role in learning what is needed to better understand. We are a team in your learning. Our job is to work together to have you achieve at high levels of success. We have a mutual responsibility to engage and make that happen. Working together will help all of us experience great success this year.

Student: So, are you saying that we don't get a grade and move on?

Teacher: What I am saying is that my job is to help you achieve and be successful. In order to do that, when you complete an assessment, together we need to make sure you understand, and as a result, we don't just move on. We make sure that we understand, and then we move on.

Student: So, we look at the results, and then what do we do?

Teacher: If you have any errors, see if you can determine why the error was made. If you can, correct it. If you don't understand, initially I will help you to find ways to learn what you need. Later in the year, you will be good at finding ways that you might do that, including using me, fellow students, parents, or other resources available to you. I am your partner in the process, so you will never be alone. At times, I will create groups to support common learning needs. Other times, you might determine a path of your own and move ahead independently.

In order to best understand, let me give to you your results. I think you will quickly see what I mean. I'd like you to think about what you did well, identify any mistakes you made, and determine if there are any areas that you don't understand. Correct mistakes and consider what might help you clear up misunderstandings.

This conversation is an initial step with students. Introduce a graphic organizer like those from chapter 4 (pages 100–101) to support student analysis. With each assessment, students will become more adept at developing and committing to their responsibility in the process. At the onset of the student analysis, teachers can share plans they have set to respond. For example, teachers may share their findings, discuss their response, and then provide students the opportunity to analyze and determine their responsibilities. That conversation might look like the following.

> Teacher: Students, I am returning to you the piece that you wrote involving stating and supporting your opinion about cell phones in school. As a whole, they were quite well written and easy to understand. Some of you have some spelling and punctuation errors that I will ask you to find and correct during your review of the results. Supporting opinions with facts is an area that I feel could be enhanced in the papers. Today during your review, I'd like you to underline the supporting facts you have included in your writing. Remember, if you stated another opinion and expect it to support the initial opinion, that doesn't count. An opinion might be something like, everyone wants a cell phone. Evidence could be a statement similar to the following: after polling the class, twenty-three out of twenty-five students felt that a cell phone was needed. Consider other ways to support your opinion with facts. You will have five minutes of class time today to brainstorm with colleagues as to how you might collect additional evidence to support your opinion. Then you will have an additional fifteen minutes to gather evidence using all resources available to you. At that point, I will ask you to independently incorporate the new evidence into your piece and correct all errors located during the rewrite.

This example is a bit more teacher directed yet engages students in the process, giving them the responsibility to improve while providing flexibility as to how that will best happen.

An alternate teacher response might include a discussion of challenge areas found in the assessment. The teacher can explain any small groups that will be formed and what the focus of each group will be. Students will understand that the groups are formed to support their learning. Although the teacher may assign students to specific groups, a volunteer situation may also be considered. During the student analysis of their data, the student may identify another way to learn what is needed and not participate in the small group. If allowing this flexibility, it will need to be clear to students that either they determine a method to learn the missed concepts, or they participate in the group. Doing nothing is not an option.

The way we word things can make a difference with students and their willingness to improve. When students experience difficulties, consider the wording you've used when speaking with them. Keeping wording as focused and positive as possible will result in a feeling of potential success rather than anger or shame. Table 5.1 provides a few examples.

Table 5.1: Wording Makes a Difference

Instead of Saying	Consider Saying
"You did this wrong."	"Take a look at your response. Do you see something you can change to improve your answer?"
"It looks like you didn't spend time on this."	"Let's have you spend a bit more time on this. Where do you think you should start in order to expand your response?"
"This is all wrong."	"In the assignment, the goal was to _____. Can you compare for me what went well and what the next steps are to reach the goal more fully?"
"You weren't listening when I explained what to do."	"Can you tell me what you were to do in order to successfully complete the assignment? What questions do you have for me?"
"Do this over."	"In order for me to best understand what you know, I'd like you to spend more time with this. What will you do to better show me that you know how to _____? What help do you need from me?"
"Your grade on this is not acceptable."	"The concepts we are working on are important to your success as we continue throughout the year. You have some good starts and are on the road to right. It is important that we look at these sections and have you rework the answers. There is a video I'd like to watch that demonstrates what to do. Is there anything else you might need to dive into the work?"
"You're not taking your work seriously."	"Why do you think we are doing this work? Can you think of ways it is important to know and do this to be more successful outside of school? What is the best next step for you in order to be successful with this work?"

Supplying Tools, Time, and Confidence

Consider methods to provide data to students. If using a traditional test format, providing students with their assessment will give them the information they need to evaluate what went well and what needs attention. In the case of a product, process, or performance, a rubric is helpful. The rubric can be returned to the student with each descriptor highlighted that accurately reflects the performance on each criterion.

Figure 5.1 is an example of a completed rubric. The symbol found in each square identifies the performance for each individual criterion listed within the rubric. If this information is provided to the student, it allows him or her to view current performance as well as what is needed to get to the next level of quality. Upon review, the student can determine next steps.

Criteria	1	2	3	4
Subject	Subject needs further explanation	Subject addressed, gaps apparent	Subject adequately addressed	✦ Subject clearly addressed including supporting details
Volume	Difficult to hear	✦ Volume erratic	Appropriate volume	Loud enough and easy to understand
Eye Contact	Lack of adequate eye contact	Erratic eye contact	✦ Intermittent eye contact	Good eye contact
Visual Aid	✦ Poor visual aid	Visual does not enhance speech	Visual helps presentation	Visual supports presentation and is used effectively
Organization	Lack of organization	Organization confusing at times	✦ Good organization	Logical organization, easy-to-follow format

Figure 5.1: Student results—rubric for giving a speech.

This student can see that the subject of the speech received the highest rating, but the organization could be improved. During the speech, volume was erratic, eye contact was intermittent, and the visual aid was poor. This may or may not be data that the teacher will choose to respond to immediately. If working on a speech unit, the student can incorporate the recommendations into his or her next speech to perform at a higher level. If at this point in the year a student needs to demonstrate proficiency, students would be required to make changes and demonstrate an enhanced performance. If class time is not available, recording the performance, presenting the speech to another group, or generating another idea to give the speech are all options.

Creating a direct connection between student performance and an immediate awareness of performance level can support student learning. When taking an assessment, consider having students evaluate the confidence they have in the accuracy and quality of their response on each assigned question, problem, or task. This can be accomplished by giving students a graphic organizer that corresponds to the number of tasks on the assessment. Take a look at figure 5.2 (page 112) for an example. The Question or Task column provides a space for each task on the assessment. While taking the assessment, students evaluate their comfort level on each task immediately after completing the item. Students evaluate their confidence and give this to the teacher with their assessment. This provides teachers with additional pieces of data. Did the students correctly respond to the concepts they felt confident about? Did the level of confidence correlate to the acceptability of the response? Does confidence positively impact the outcome? This information is useful to the teacher, and students as well. As possible, the teacher can evaluate the level of confidence prior to administering an assessment to ensure that students are ready to accurately demonstrate understanding. After assessments are scored and returned, the student evaluation is given back to the students so the two can be compared. Students can evaluate their level of confidence compared to the results. Students can also see the connection between confidence and performance. Self-evaluation will provide evidence that confidence in their understanding leads to enhanced results. Confidence is gained through attentiveness, engagement, involvement, performance, and on-task behavior. All are qualities we want students to exhibit.

Set the expectation. Students need to be aware that they are integral players in the learning process. Implement the time, teaching, and action approach. Students will become experts at evaluating their own performance. They are also likely to take learning more seriously on the front end so that their initial assessment performance demonstrates proficiency with little or no response required.

Students, place an X in the column that best reflects how you feel about each task on the assessment.							
Question or Task	I don't understand this.	I guessed.	I did this well.	Question or Task	I don't understand this.	I guessed.	I did this well.
1				6			
2				7			
3				8			
4				9			
5				10			

Figure 5.2: Student evaluation of confidence during assessment.

Allowing Students to Track Progress

Students can track progress in different ways. In many schools, students have access to their grades and can track them online. In some classes, teachers have students plot their scores on a graph, so they are able to visualize overall progress. Many teachers conference with students to share progress over time. Often when we consider tracking student progress, it is summative progress. Instead, let's consider a more detailed approach. The goal to having students involved is so they are able to tell what they did well, what they need to work on, and what role they will play in the process. If they only track global scores, they just may know they need to improve, but there is no specificity. For example, if students plot the percentage score they received on mathematics tests during a portion of the year, they may have a graph that looks something like figure 5.3.

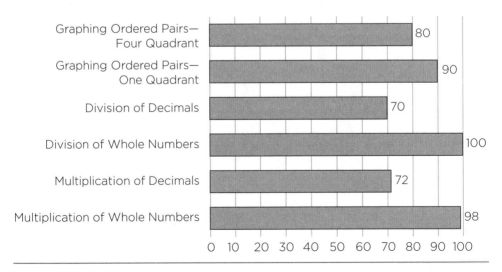

Figure 5.3: Mathematics test scores.

As a student, I can see on which tests I received a better score. However, it doesn't tell me what I did well, what I misunderstood, and how I responded. It also appears final. A score is recorded, and I'm done with it. That is not the message we want to send. An analysis of the actual performance provides the detail needed for improvement. Creating a plan to improve sends the message that misunderstandings are not left unaddressed. The goal is not the score; the goal is continued learning.

Student portfolios can help students understand, respond to, and evaluate growth based on assessment performance. Initially, teachers will need to guide students through the purpose and format of the portfolio. Throughout the year, they will have assessments to add to the portfolio. Periodically, students will need opportunities to reflect on their progress.

The student assessment portfolio can include the assessment, their reflection on the assessment, any work that shows an increased level of performance on concepts originally misunderstood, and periodic, possibly quarterly, reflections on growth over time. Figure 5.4 provides a template as a record and brief reflection tool. The purpose is to record all additions to the portfolio and include thoughts as to why it is included. Figure 5.5 (page 114) is a student example.

Student Name:		
Item Added	Date Added	Reflection

Figure 5.4: Portfolio record sheet.

An approach to organize and store assessment results, the students' planned responses to their results, and evidence supporting their new learning will help students to track their progress throughout the year. If portfolios are to work effectively, they need to become systematic. The assessment is returned and

Student Name:		
Item Added	**Date Added**	**Reflection**
Finding Area Assessment	2/17	I found that on the assessment I could find the area of the shapes really well. I had trouble finding the area of an unusual shape. I forgot that I can divide the unusual shape into shapes I know, find the areas, then add them up.
My Response to the Area Assessment	2/18	I added a copy of my assessment response to keep a record of what I said I would do to improve my performance. My teacher also mentioned a video I could watch to help me better understand.
Evidence to Support New Learning on the Area Assessment	2/25	This is an example of different problems I did to find the area of an unusual shape. The first shape I was able to split into a combination of rectangles and triangles. The second shape I used all triangles to find the total area.
Finding the Area of Trapezoids Assessment	3/15	I did really well on this test and didn't have any mistakes or misunderstandings. The teacher also added some unusual shapes to the end of the assessment, and I could do those too.
My Response to the Trapezoid Assessment	3/16	I added this because it is a celebration. I understand and was able to show what I know. I won't include a response because I don't need to do a response since I did so well.
Area Performance Task Rubric	3/18	This rubric shows what I did on the area task. All of my scores are threes and fours. In the future, I need to watch how I organize information to make it easier to understand.

Figure 5.5: Student example—portfolio record sheet.

placed in the portfolio. The student completes his or her response to the assessment (see figure 5.5) and inserts it into the portfolio. The student carries out the work outlined in the response and places evidence into the portfolio that demonstrates his or her new learning. Teachers will need to provide time and instruction to students if the portfolio is to become an automatic approach. When the assessment is returned, a simple reminder is given. "Let's take out our portfolios and place the assessment inside. Take a few minutes to add it to the record sheet."

Quarterly, or at times that coincide with report cards, students should review their portfolio to reflect on their performance. Figure 5.6 provides an example.

Instructions: Students, the purpose of this reflection is to review your work over time. In your reflection, consider sharing the following: strengths, challenges, progress you have made, examples of what you have done to overcome challenges, and things you are proud of.

Date: *October 30*

Reflection:

I looked through my work since the beginning of the year. I always worry about my writing because it isn't easy for me. I started out getting ones and twos on the rubric, but the rubric helped me know what I needed to do to improve. It also helped that my teacher held small groups to work on how to write an introduction. She even shared some links to videos on YouTube that gave advice. Now I do my own searches on YouTube when I'm stuck even before I turn in an assignment. That works for me because I do better the first time and don't have much to respond to.

I'm happy with the progress I've made, but I know I need to continue to get better. Right now, even though I've improved, I am getting mostly threes. I need to work on supplying evidence to claims, and I also need to work on writing better conclusions. Sometimes I just end. I don't conclude.

Figure 5.6: Cumulative portfolio reflection.

Student-led conferences will add importance to maintaining a quality portfolio. Portfolios assist students as they take responsibility for sharing performance and progress with parents. Students have evidence from everything they learned and proof of the active role they played in the learning process. Teachers can provide students with a portfolio record sheet, such as the one in figure 5.7 (page 116), to help guide them through their conference.

Description of Work	Date Assigned	Strengths Exhibited	Areas for Improvement
Describe the work, including the purpose of the assignment.		Identify the strengths you illustrated, defining the purpose and how you fulfilled that purpose.	Highlight any areas in which you could improve. Be specific in your intended actions or describe what you might do differently if given the same assignment again.
Piece 1:			
Piece 2:			
Piece 3:			
Piece 4:			
Piece 5:			
Summative reflection: Summarize your work overall reflecting on growth, strengths, and challenges, as well as your next steps to experience continued growth.			

Figure 5.7: Student portfolio record sheet.

Parents are not always available for conferences, and depending on the age of the students, attendance varies. Consider conducting a portfolio-sharing session with volunteer adults from the school or district. Students can be scheduled into short sharing sessions during which they meet with volunteer teachers or district administrators who will actively listen to the student. Students should also share the portfolio with their teacher on a periodic basis. Spot-checking the portfolio will also ensure that students are fulfilling portfolio expectations.

Portfolios actively engage students in their learning and promote self-generated responses to their own data. Student progress is validated, and the importance of the portfolio is clear. The portfolio is evidence of progress and commitment to student learning.

Setting Goals as a Response to Data

Up until this point we have considered student involvement in data analysis, reflection, and response to data. As part of the response, student goal-setting is a valuable option. It adds an additional factor to the process which already involves students considering what they want to accomplish in advance and setting goals to reach their intended outcomes. Setting of goals will provide additional purpose to the other data response components highlighted in this chapter.

A simple but thoughtful process is useful. Consider the time available to support student goal-setting. Choose a time frame that works. Are students setting goals that are based on a period of learning like a chapter, unit, quarter, or semester? Will time be provided to monitor goal progress? Is the time period long enough so that students have multiple opportunities to review their progress? Will there be suggestions on what the content of the goal will encompass?

The system of data review is already in place when using a portfolio or a system of assessment analysis and response. A goal review can be incorporated into the review process with limited additional effort or time. Students review their goals as they analyze assessment results. Figure 5.8 (page 118) provides an example.

The student example in figure 5.8 shares a goal set for the first quarter in her mathematics class. She has used a report card grade as her goal. Although a grade does not provide details as to how a student performed on any given assessment, the detailed approach suggested in this chapter has students review their work in its entirety. Students review the results and commit to actions they will take to gain a deeper understanding if their performance suggests the need. Simultaneously, the teacher also shares the response planned for the class. The two combined make it clear that the goal of the assessment is not the grade; the goal is understanding the standards, content, and learning targets. The grade is a reality, though, and is a helpful data point on which to set a goal.

Linking Data to Action

Students' involvement in a response to their learning is crucial to the learning process. Learning doesn't end. Performance is never final. Continued growth is

Name: *Belle*	
Clearly state your goal. What do you want to accomplish? By when?	*By the end of this quarter, I want to get at least a B in mathematics.*
Outline steps you will take to achieve your goal.	*In order to reach my goal, I will (1) pay attention in class, (2) do any work for the class on time, (3) study and apply myself, and (4) ask questions and follow directions.*
What will success look like?	*I will do well on a daily basis, and if not, I'll get help. I will pass tests.*
Include the date and a brief description of progress following each assessment.	**Date:** *September 15* **Progress:** *I did okay on the first test but found that I didn't understand a whole section. The teacher has us look at our results and gives us a chance to learn more and show that we now understand. This will help me to achieve my goal. I plan on asking others what was expected in the section I missed. I am also creating a plan to redo the work. I found a video that helps me understand the procedure. It will help me not only complete the section but do it successfully.* **Date:** **Progress:** **Date:** **Progress:**

Figure 5.8: Sample student goal-setting form.

an expectation for all students, and they are the key players in making it happen. Student involvement sets the stage for self-reliance and helps students to understand they are truly in charge of their destinies.

Students who struggle need to continue in rigorous courses and be supported rather than placed indefinitely into remedial courses. Support in rigorous coursework increases the probability that the student will experience success in future classes and courses (Sanders, Jurich, Mittapalli, & Taylor, 2013). When students are aware of their responsibilities in the process and know that the expectation for success revolves around their involvement and commitment to learning, the opportunity to be successful increases. Teachers can set the stage and support student involvement and growth through creating a system of student engagement and accountability in their learning.

To turn data into action, consider the following questions.

- What ways do you suggest building confidence in students so they feel capable of understanding and responding to their assessment results?

- How do you report results to students? How do you suggest helping students understand their data?

- Students take ownership when they track and use their data. What ways do you incorporate this practice in your classroom?

CHAPTER 6

Considering Sustainability

A systematic approach to assessment, data review, and action provides expanded opportunities for students to learn and grow. Student performance on assessments causes us to review and react according to student need. We involve students in the process to support their journey to become lifelong learners.

In this chapter, we look at sustainability and consider some practices that support all processes and techniques previously mentioned in this book, yet they are not specifically tied to responding to student data. Instead, these considerations surround practices that support the long-term success of a systematic approach to responding to student results.

Connecting with parents or guardians to develop a collaborative relationship with them and the student is a valuable component of sustaining student success. We'll also look at the benefit of providing students with a variety of assessment types and opportunities to show what they know. Additionally, how students are taught impacts the way they learn. Therefore, the chapter explores the selection and use of strategies. Being aware of a strategy's effectiveness supports student learning. Lastly, a section on administrative support describes leaders' influential role in student learning.

Parent Support

Parents can be our greatest allies regardless of the age of the student. They want what is best for their child and appreciate understanding how each teacher supports student growth and academic performance. In his book *Visible Learning*, John Hattie (2009) shares that parents are very capable of assisting and supporting schools, but they need to understand how that is possible. Parents need to, as Hattie (2009) puts it, "learn the language of schooling" so they are capable of supporting the growth of their child (p. 33). Shared expectations assist in student growth. Lack of parent understanding can create counterproductive environments. Shared expectations assist in student growth.

Connect with parents to create an awareness of the approach to assessment being used within your classroom. Parents are likely most familiar with practices used when they were in school. This may have been a system that relied heavily on lengthy summative assessments, followed by a letter grade or percentage calculated from the performance, followed by moving on to the next chapter or unit of study. Responsibilities for learning have changed. We are no longer in a world where assigning a grade and moving on is acceptable. The current state of education requires a shared responsibility for student learning and performance. So that students reach their optimum level of learning, a response to data has become a matter of course.

So, what might parents need to know? They will benefit from knowing the structure of the system of assessment in the classroom. It should be simply stated but informative. Parents should know that students are frequently assessed in order to identify any misunderstandings before they become a significant problem for the students. Concepts are assessed individually and cumulatively. Students will be asked to take an active role in their learning, which will include participating in relearning activities and practices when misunderstandings are evident. When mistakes occur, students may be asked to correct them in order to prove and solidify understanding. Students and teacher are a team, and students will take an active role in their learning with expectations that include involvement in evaluating their individual strengths and challenges. Students and the teacher alike will take part in clearing up misunderstandings so that achievement can soar. Students will keep track of their data. They will be aware of and reflect on their growth over time. Parent support in these processes is appreciated. Parents are key players in the educational process, and their support will impact student results.

Multiple methods of contact will increase the chances that many or most parents are aware of the identified assessment procedures. Use whatever sources of contact are available in your situation. Early in the year, many schools have parent nights during which parents have the opportunity to meet teachers and provide information to those who are able to attend. Teacher websites offer a location on which to post information. Students can be given the information and asked to share it with their parents. Email is an effective vehicle to make a connection. Teacher newsletters, parent conferences, letters home, phone calls, and any other available sources can be considered to determine their potential effectiveness (see figure 6.1). Figure 6.1 shares an example of a letter to parents. The assessment process could also be included with additional information. Weigh the options. If the letter becomes too lengthy, wordy, or filled with educational jargon, it is not likely to have the intended impact and may not even be read.

Keeping Informed

Mrs. Smith's School-Home Connection Newsletter

This Week's Topic: Assessment

In our classroom, the word *assessment* refers to anything students are asked to do to demonstrate their understanding of the things we are learning in the classroom. The pattern that we follow in the classroom includes instruction, student engagement in activities to support the new concepts being learned, a practice activity, and then a brief test to determine how well the concepts were understood.

Over time the students will also be assessed on more than one concept at the same time. For example, after a few days of learning, there might be a brief test given on what students have learned. Throughout the year, there will also be chapter and unit tests. My goal is to assess often, so if there are misunderstandings, we can catch them early in order for students to experience the highest levels of success.

After each assessment, I will analyze the results and work with students to clarify any misunderstandings that occurred. We will engage in reteaching and additional practice when concepts that are misunderstood are crucial to future success. This will not inhibit progress, but instead support learning and student engagement and commitment to their success.

As always, I appreciate your support and encourage your questions. Thank you for taking an active and encouraging role in your child's education.

Figure 6.1: Sample parent newsletter.

Keeping parents in the know increases the probability that parents will be supportive. The system of responding to data may be unfamiliar to parents. As a result, explaining the systematic approach to assessment in advance of using it in the classroom will provide parents with a basic understanding of what to expect and how the system works. It will not be a surprise to those who are unfamiliar with the need or purpose for these types of procedures.

Parents could also use a questionnaire, such as the one in figure 6.2 (page 124), to further their involvement with students' learning. Questions, or discussion starters, encourage student-parent communication. If they have concerns, bring students' answers to these questions to any parent-teacher meeting.

Assessment Variety

In order to elicit the best possible student performance, a variety of assessment types should be considered. When students are allowed to show what they know in a variety of ways, there is a greater likelihood that they will demonstrate understanding. Multiple methods limit the impact of confusion students may experience when demonstrating knowledge in specific and repeated formats. For example, if lengthy multiple-choice tests are the most common form

Directions: Choose one question to ask your child or children each week. If desired, include the subject that you would like the student to concentrate on for their response. Add your own to stimulate thoughtful discussions about school.

1. What's one thing you learned today, and why do you think it is important to the subject?
2. What did you find difficult in school today? What makes it hard for you?
3. Tell me one thing you did today that you really enjoyed. What made it enjoyable?
4. What careers are likely to use the skills you are learning in _____ (subject)?
5. If you were going to make a test in _____ (subject) on the things you learned today, what are two questions you would ask? What would a correct answer be to the questions?
6. Teachers use a variety of ways to teach. What did a teacher do today that you felt really helped you learn?
7. What are the three most important things you learned today?
8. If you could have done one thing differently in school today, what would it be?
9. What subject do you feel most confident in? Why is that the case?
10. If you were asked to teach one of your classes today, which one would it be, and why?
11. When you take a test, what kinds of tests do you prefer, and why?
12. How do you think you best prepare for a test?
13. What made you feel confident when you did your schoolwork today? What concerns did you have?
14. How do you feel you are doing in _____ (subject)? How do you know?
15. What did you feel good about in school today? Why?

Other Questions You Might Like to Ask

Figure 6.2: Questions to encourage parent involvement.

*Visit **go.SolutionTree.com/assessment** for a reproducible version of this figure.*

of assessment and students find them difficult, tedious, or confusing, they are not likely to demonstrate their understanding effectively even if they are familiar and comfortable with the content.

The goal is to give the assessment in formats that provide students with the best opportunity to show what they know. Consider all options available to appropriately evaluate the learning targets and provide variety and choice. Multiple methods can be employed throughout a unit of study to provide students the best chance to demonstrate understanding. Table 6.1 shares a variety of options. Also consider the hints provided within chapter 2.

Table 6.1: Test-Design Options

Items Requiring the Identification or Selection of a Response	Items Requiring the Construction of a Response
Multiple choice	Provide evidence
True or false	Project
Labeling	Performance
Matching	Speech
Fill-in-the-blank	Discussion
Time line	Conversation
Defining	Conference
Select best approach	Interview
	Teach

The levels of difficulty with each type of question vary depending on the sophistication of the question. In fact, in most cases, a constructed response can be turned into a selected response and vice versa. Questions that ask students to identify, or select, a response are those where the correct answer is present along with answers that are not correct. Students select the best answer or answers from a list. Constructing a response requires the student to use his or her knowledge and skills to formulate a correct answer without answer choices being available. For example, a constructed-response example might ask students to list and explain the primary factors that impact the formation of a hurricane, whereas in a selected-response assessment, students might have to choose all the correct responses from a list of wind, rain, low pressure, water vapor, all of the above, and none of the above.

Selection and Use of Strategies

Throughout the previous chapters, it has been suggested that the teaching strategies used be reviewed and connected to the level of student performance on the assessment. The intent of this section is not to teach strategies, but to spur thought and suggest resources.

How did the strategies impact the intended outcome? Was the strategy effective? What strategies will be used for reteaching to eliminate misunderstandings? What teaching methods inspired the best results? What alternative methods can be considered to teach the same learning targets? What do my colleagues suggest?

Consider methods to introduce information and procedures to students. Evaluate the impact of direct instruction, group activities, audio-visual presentations, web-based research, teamwork, engaging tasks, projects, performances, and other methods used.

In the book *Classroom Instruction That Works*, Robert Marzano, Debra Pickering, and Jane Pollock (2001) review and recommend the following nine strategies.

1. Identifying similarities and differences
2. Summarizing and note taking
3. Reinforcing effort and providing recognition
4. Homework and practice
5. Using nonlinguistic representations
6. Engaging students in cooperative learning
7. Setting objectives and providing feedback
8. Generating and testing hypotheses
9. Using cues, questions, and advanced organizers

Assessment strategies can also impact learning. Preassessment can help identify those concepts students already know as well as those they need to learn. Allow students to demonstrate understanding multiple times as necessary to reflect a successful outcome, and consider the most recent demonstration a replacement to the former less, successful performances. Clear identification of learning goals will support student success when goals are apparent to the teacher and the students. Early and ongoing feedback provided to students impacts learning because it assists students in knowing how their performance compares to the identified goal while also providing support in how to advance to the desired outcome (McTighe & O'Connor, 2005).

Students who understand how learning relates directly to them are more likely to be successful. When the purpose of the learning is clearly defined, and it is related to life outside the classroom, value and meaning are added to the experience. As important, if students feel that they can actually be successful, they are more likely to experience success (McTighe, 2000).

Literally hundreds of resources are available that highlight and specifically address teaching strategies. Review the bank of approaches used in your classroom, consider adding to the assortment, and vary the approaches used within and among lessons. Get feedback from students to best understand the connection between the instructional strategies and how they impacted student understanding. As we grow the bank of strategies in our toolkit, we increase our choices and best match learning targets to teaching strategies.

Administrator Support

Strong leadership supports teachers' ability to build capacity and understand assessment design, implementation, analysis, and action. "Effective use of data may depend on several enabling factors including strong leadership, up-front planning for data collection and use, and strong human capacity for data-driven inquiry" (Kerr et al., 2006, p. 498).

At times, it seems as though teachers have an unlimited capacity, knowledge, and drive. What is limited, however, is time—time to learn and grow, time to know where to place efforts and where to let go. Administrative vision and support can provide welcome guidance. Creating and implementing a professional development plan to provide time and training will grow the expertise of teachers and improve student learning.

To best support teachers' efforts and support a quality assessment development, implementation, and response to data cycle, a school learning plan is beneficial. Think of it as you would a lesson plan that is extended throughout the year and preferable over multiple years for the best possibility of long-term success. Figure 6.3 (page 128) provides a sample template and some short- and long-term goals to consider. Although it is listed as a three-year plan, it is one that will need to continue. New teachers will require an introduction to the structure and systematic approach to assessment. Existing teachers will benefit from time, support, and collaboration in order to continue to embed and systematize that which was previously learned.

The goals on the template are followed by space for detailed action steps that have been identified to reach the goals for each year of the plan. In this area, specific information is included and defined well in advance of implementation. The specific actions stated are followed with measures of success. In other words, how will it be determined if the action step was a success? Assigning names to the action will help get the job done. An implementation date guarantees time is set aside for the action to occur.

With any professional development implementation or teacher learning experience, consider an approach I like to call *take away, bring back*. The learning experience itself should include ample opportunity for teacher engagement, practice, and creation. With that in mind, the recommendation is to set a time frame for the actual use of the information and tools created during professional

Long-term goal: By the end of the three-year implementation, teachers will have a systematic approach to the quality design of standards-based assessments that will lead to actionable data.

Short-term goals:

Year one—Capture all professional learning days for the following.

1. Learn about and understand assessment as a cycle.
2. Gain a common and detailed understanding of an approach to deconstruct standards.
3. Understand assessment design and create quality assessments based on the standards that will lead to quality, actionable data.

Year two—Capture all professional learning days for the following.

1. Continue embedding the work from year one.
2. Learn more about and share ideas regarding the collecting, organizing, and interpreting of data.

Year three—Capture all professional learning days for the following.

1. Continue to embed the work of years one and two.
2. Concentrate on the response to data. Share ideas, and create learning opportunities.
3. Create classroom and school structures that support implementing a response to essential data.

Specific Actions to Achieve Short- and Long-Term Goals			
Action Steps	**Measures of Success**	**Person or People Responsible for Research and Implementation**	**Date of Initial Implementation**
Plan Details—Year One			
Learn about and understand assessment as a cycle.	Teachers will be able to identify and use an assessment cycle independently and with their collaborative team.	Team leaders at each grade level and in each department will identify those who will research. All are responsible for implementation.	September 10
Gain a common and detailed understanding of an approach to deconstruct standards.	All teachers will have a common approach to the deconstruction of standards. Teachers will use this approach in teams and independently.	Principal will provide approach.	November 1

Understand assessment design and create quality assessments based on the standards that will lead to quality, actionable data.	Teachers and teams will design assessments and share them at faculty meetings to demonstrate proficiency and share great ideas.	Team leaders	February 1
Anticipated Plan Details—Year Two			
Continue to embed the work of years one and two.	Share sessions at faculty meetings, and observe team meetings.	Principal, leadership team, team leaders, all teachers	October 1
Learn more about and share ideas regarding the collecting, organizing, and interpreting of data.	Choose and read one book per semester that promotes the goal.	Team leader	October 1 and February 1
Anticipated Plan Details—Year Three			
Continue to embed the work of years one and two.	Data discussions occur during faculty meetings and meetings. The plan is the focus of all professional learning days.	Principal and leadership team	First day of school
Concentrate on the response to data. Share ideas and create learning opportunities.	This is the sole work of collaborative teams. Data discussions occur during faculty meetings and meetings. The plan is the focus of all professional learning days.	Team leaders and all teachers	October 1
Create classroom and school structures that support implementing a response to essential data.	Data discussions occur during faculty meetings and meetings. The plan is the focus of all professional learning days.	Principal and leadership team	February 1

Figure 6.3: School or district three-year assessment professional development plan.

*Visit **go.SolutionTree.com/assessment** for a reproducible version of this figure.*

development. Then, during a follow-up faculty meeting or collaborative team discussion, set the stage for sharing and discussion of the implementation. What specifically did you use? What was the outcome? What successes can you share? Do you have recommendations for the future?

Any specific information that teachers provide will help administrators understand classroom and school needs. It's important to share data throughout the year from a variety of assessments to gather evidence. Classroom, grade level, school, and state assessments can all play an active role in determining student need. Although state assessments are often further removed from the classroom, the data support school and district findings. When teachers identify common difficulties within and across grade levels, the data indicate a potential problem. Is there a root cause? Perhaps the concepts aren't addressed within the resources. The timing of the teaching may need adjusting. The teacher's methods used could need adjusting. Regardless of the cause, administrator awareness should result in action in regard to reaching the school's or district's goals. This often includes leaders adjusting resources and budgets.

The goals in figure 6.3 are ambitious, but they can be accomplished if time and expertise support them. Although it is often difficult to maintain a limited focus, implementation is more likely to be successful with fewer goals. Doug Reeves (2011) suggests that schools should have no more than six goals, and they should be clearly focused on student needs. In addition, professional development linked to the goals and administrative support and monitoring will influence the level of success (Reeves, 2011).

Goal development provides focus for teachers, teams, and administrators. What do school data indicate as a need? What direction do our district goals promote? What are our professional development needs for the school? Where do the responses of all three questions intersect?

Consider the following eight steps when developing goals.

1. Identify the area of need considering school and district data as well as any predetermined district and school focus.

2. Determine the school's needs, and select the desired focus areas from step one.

3. Keep in mind the available budget.

4. Evaluate the time available to promote new learning related to the goal as well as the implementation of the goals.

5. Be realistic in the number of years it will take to solidify the intended outcome. Plan for a multiple-year implementation.

6. Limit the number of goals.

7. Know the intended outcomes and develop a plan to specifically address the goals.

8. Monitor the implementation and results throughout the year. Adjust the plan as necessary to continue a dedicated focus.

Successfully implementing any initiative does not happen just because professional development is provided. We all know this. There are, however, components that support a successful implementation. In a research study conducted in 2011, teachers were asked to identify components that will most likely lead them from learning to implementation. Three factors surfaced to the top of the list. Administrative support and expectation added to the likelihood that the learning would be implemented in the classroom. Teachers also believed that if the learning goals were a focus of their colleagues and if they had the opportunity to collaborate with others, practices would become a reality (Depka, 2012).

Linking Data to Action

This chapter considered sustaining the foundation that supports an effective response to data. Building close relationships with parents adds to educators' ability to include them as an integral part of a data response system. Using a variety of assessment types creates a well-rounded picture of student successes and challenges. Students have the opportunity to respond with methods they are comfortable using. If a method blocks their ability to respond, they are able to show their understanding in another way either on the same assessment or at a different point in time. Teaching strategies should have a positive impact on student learning. We don't always know what the impact will be. In fact, a strategy that works perfectly one year may not work at all the next. Having a large toolbox of strategies is most effective. Students are teachers' best source when it comes to knowing the effectiveness of strategies. If we not only use the strategy but fill the students in on what the strategy is and why we are using it, students will be able to provide feedback as to its success. Administrators play a crucial role in teacher support. Teachers benefit from the data administrators supply regarding student strengths, challenges, and needs. A clear and focused path of goal attainment will support student success. This collaborative effort between administration and staff can have a direct impact on student success.

To turn data into action, consider the following questions.

- How do you currently gain parents' and guardians' support? What practices might you add?

- How can you expand student understanding of the strategies you use by explaining what they are and why you use them? What questions can you ask students to help them evaluate which strategies had the biggest impact on their understanding?

- What do you and your colleagues do to keep administrators informed of classroom practices and data associated with student success? Are there practices you will consider adding?

EPILOGUE: CLOSING THOUGHTS

The thoughts highlighted and approaches identified within this book are part of a system. Although single practices that were suggested can be useful, a systematic view of the contents is recommended. In order to successfully respond to student needs, we look to the very beginning of the goals being taught and consider all seven of the steps that follow.

1. Identify the standards and targets of the unit. Determine priority learning outcomes.

2. Build assessments to address identified standards and learning targets. Stress priority outcomes.

3. Determine strategies and methods to use for instruction. Design lessons.

4. Assess students throughout the unit. Collect, organize, and make sense of data.

5. A systematic approach and expectation will have the best results. Create a culture of data use and analysis.

6. Distinguish between what is and is not essential. Decide on strategies needed to respond to essential outcomes.

7. Implement, assess, and measure the effectiveness of the responses on students.

In addition, recall from chapter 4 that a response to data is essential:

- **If** the standard is important to the subject during the current school year

- **And** the standard is important to other subjects during the current school year

- **And** the standard is important throughout school years

- **And** the standard is important to college, career, and life

Finally, the response to data begins at the earliest stages of standards identification and unit development. The questions that are asked of students correspond directly to the targets of the lesson. The alignment between the question and the concept identifies the response needed should confusion arise. Concepts are assessed in combination as well, but it is the assessment of individual concepts that help identify student strengths and misunderstandings. Consider the following steps during assessment development to create a tool designed to elicit informative data.

1. Clearly identify targets from standards, portions of standards, and content.

2. Create questions or tasks clearly aligned to each part of each target.

3. Design lessons specific to the targets identified.

4. Assess students. Complete an item, section, or rubric analysis of the assessment.

5. Review the analysis, and plan lessons to address high-priority areas of concern.

A systematic approach to assessment design supports the probability of quality informative data. It is data and question alignment that lead to actionable results, leading to enhanced student achievement.

REFERENCES AND RESOURCES

Ainsworth, L. (2007). Common formative assessments: The centerpiece of an integrated standards-based assessment system. In D. Reeves (Ed.), *Ahead of the curve: The power of assessment to transform teaching and learning* (pp. 79–101). Bloomington, IN: Solution Tree Press.

Allen, R. (2005, August). *Using the evidence of student achievement for improvements at individual, class, and school level.* Presented at the conference of the Australian Council for Educational Research, Melbourne, Victoria, Australia. Accessed at https://research.acer.edu.au/cgi/viewcontent.cgi?article=1000&context=research_conference_2005 on January 11, 2018.

Boudett, K. P., City, E. A., & Murnane, R. J. (Eds.). (2013). *Data wise: A step-by-step guide to using assessment results to improve teaching and learning.* Cambridge, MA: Harvard Education Press.

Buffum, A., Mattos, M., & Malone, J. (2018). *Taking action: A handbook for RTI at Work.* Bloomington, IN: Solution Tree Press.

Burke, K., & Depka, E. (2011). *Using formative assessment in the RTI framework.* Bloomington, IN: Solution Tree Press.

Campbell, C., & Levin, B. (2008). *Using data to support educational improvement.* Accessed at http://wiafterschoolnetwork.org/wp-content/uploads/2016/08/Using-Data-to-Support-Educational-Improvement.pdf on May 7, 2018.

Darling-Hammond, L. (2006). Constructing 21st-century teacher education. *Journal of Teacher Education, 57*(3), 300–314.

Datnow, A. (2017). *Opening or closing doors for students? Equity and data-driven decision-making.* Accessed at https://research.acer.edu.au/cgi/viewcontent.cgi?article=1317&context=research_conference on May 8, 2018.

Depka, E. (2012). *From professional development to implementation: What teachers say makes change happen.* Unpublished doctoral dissertation, Cardinal Stritch University, Milwaukee, WI.

Depka, E. (2015). *Bringing homework into focus: Tools and tips to enhance practices, design, and feedback.* Bloomington, IN: Solution Tree Press.

Depka, E. (2017). *Raising the rigor: Effective questioning strategies and techniques for the classroom.* Bloomington, IN: Solution Tree Press.

DuFour, R., DuFour, R., Eaker, R., Many, T. W., & Mattos, M. (2016). *Learning by doing: A handbook for Professional Learning Communities at Work* (3rd ed.). Bloomington, IN: Solution Tree Press.

Erkens, C., Schimmer, T., & Vagle, N. D. (2017). *Essential assessment: Six tenets for bringing hope, efficacy, and achievement to the classroom.* Bloomington, IN: Solution Tree Press.

FutureEd. (2017). *Paper versus online testing. What's the impact on test scores?* Accessed at www.future-ed.org/work/paper-vs-online-testing-whats-the-impact-on-test-scores on December 25, 2018.

Gallagher, L., Means, B., & Padilla, C. (2008). *Teachers' use of student data systems to improve instruction: 2005 to 2007.* Accessed at www2.ed.gov/rschstat/eval/tech/teachers-data-use-2005–2007/teachers-data-use-2005–2007.pdf on August 6, 2018.

Guerriero, S. (n.d.). *Teachers' pedagogical knowledge and the teaching profession.* Accessed at www.oecd.org/education/ceri/Background_document_to_Symposium_ITEL-FINAL.pdf on May 7, 2018.

Guskey, T. (2007). Using assessments to improve teaching and learning. In D. Reeves (Ed.), *Ahead of the curve: The power of assessment to transform teaching and learning* (pp. 15–29). Bloomington, IN: Solution Tree Press.

Hamilton, L., Halverson, R., Jackson, S. S., Mandinach, E., Supovitz, J. A., & Wayman, J. C. (2009). *Using student achievement data to support instructional decision making.* Washington, DC: National Center for Education Evaluation and Regional Assistance, Institute of Education Sciences, & U.S. Department of Education. Accessed at https://ies.ed.gov/ncee/wwc/Docs/PracticeGuide/dddm_pg_092909.pdf on May 7, 2018.

Hattie, J. (2009). *Visible learning: A synthesis of over 800 meta-analyses relating to achievement.* Abingdon, England: Routledge.

Hong, C. E., & Lawrence, S. A. (2011). Action research in teacher education: Classroom inquiry, reflection, and data-driven decision making. *Journal of Inquiry & Action in Education, 4*(2), 1–17.

Kerr, K. A., Marsh, J. A., Ikemoto, G. S., Darilek, H., & Barney, H. (2006). Strategies to promote data use for instructional improvement: Actions, outcomes, and lessons from three urban districts. *American Journal of Education, 112*(4), 496–520.

Lachat, M. A., & Smith, S. (2005). Practices that support data use in urban high schools. *Journal of Education for Students Placed at Risk, 10*(3), 333–349.

Mandinach, E. B., Honey, M., & Light, D. (2006, April). *A theoretical framework for data-driven decision making.* Paper presented at the annual meeting of the American Educational Research Association, San Francisco.

Marsh, J. A., Pane, J. F., & Hamilton, L. S. (2006). *Making sense of data-driven decision making in education.* Accessed at www.rand.org/content/dam/rand/pubs/occasional_papers/2006/RAND_OP170.pdf on January 12, 2018.

Marzano, R., Pickering D., & Pollock, J. E. (2001). *Classroom instruction that works: Research-based strategies for increasing student achievement.* Alexandria, VA: Association for Supervision and Curriculum Development.

McTighe, J. (2000). Meaningful learning for all students. *California Professional Development Consortia, 24,* 1–5.

McTighe, J., & O'Connor, K. (2005). Seven practices for effective learning. *Educational Leadership, 63*(3), 10–17.

Means, B., Chen, E., DeBarger, A., & Padilla, C. (2011). *Teachers' ability to use data to inform instruction: Challenges and supports.* Washington, DC: U.S. Department of Education.

Midgley, S., Stringfield, S., & Wauman, J. (2006, April). *Leadership for data-based decision-making: Collaborative educator teams.* Paper presented at the annual meeting of the American Educational Research Association, San Francisco.

National Governors Association Center for Best Practices & Council of Chief State School Officers. (2010a). *Common Core State Standards for English language arts and literacy in history/social studies, science, and technical subjects.* Washington, DC: Authors. Accessed at www.corestandards.org/assets/CCSSI_ELA%20Standards.pdf on December 21, 2018.

National Governors Association Center for Best Practices & Council of Chief State School Officers. (2010b). *Common Core State Standards for mathematics*. Washington, DC: Authors. Accessed at www.corestandards .org/assets/CCSSI_Math%20Standards.pdf on December 21, 2018.

Popham, W. J. (2008). *Classroom assessment: What teachers need to know*. Boston: Pearson.

Protheroe, N. (2009). *Improving teaching and learning with data-based decisions: Asking the right questions and acting on the answers*. Accessed at www .rogersschools.net/common/pages/DisplayFile.aspx?itemId=3497164 on January 12, 2018.

Reeves, D. (2011). For effective leadership, limit initiatives and link professional development. *ASCD Express, 7*(6). Accessed at www.ascd.org/ascd-express /vol7/706-video.aspx on May 17, 2018.

Renshaw, P., Baroutsis, A., Van Kraayenoord, C., Goos, M., & Dole, S. (2013). *Teachers using classroom data well: Identifying key features and effective practices*. Brisbane, Queensland, Australia: University of Queensland.

Sanders, K., Jurich, S., Mittapalli, K., & Taylor, L. (2013). *Identifying successful practices for students with disabilities in Ohio schools: Evidence-based practices in special education—A review of the literature*. Accessed at www.ocecd.org /Downloads/Redesign_Literature_Review_July_2013.pdf on January 12, 2018.

Schifter, C. C., Natarajan, U., Ketelhut, D. J., & Kirchgessner, A. (2014). Data-driven decision making: Facilitating teacher use of student data to inform classroom instruction. *Contemporary Issues in Technology and Teacher Education, 14*(4), 419–432.

Schmoker, M. (2011). *Focus: Elevating the essentials to radically improve student learning*. Alexandria, VA: Association for Supervision and Curriculum Development.

Shorr, P. W. (2003). *10 things you always wanted to know about data-driven decision making*. Accessed at www.scholastic.com/browse/article.jsp?id=423 on January 12, 2018.

Singley, M. K., & Lam, R. B. (2005). *The classroom sentinel: Supporting data-driven decision-making in the classroom*. Accessed at wwwconference .org/2005a/cdrom/docs/p315.pdf on January 12, 2018.

Spillane, J. P. (2012). Data in practice: Conceptualizing the data-based decision-making phenomena. *American Journal of Education, 118*(2), 113–141. Accessed at www.journals.uchicago.edu/doi/abs/10.1086/663283 on January 12, 2018.

Stefanou, C. R., Perencevich, K. C., DiCintio, M., & Turner, J. C. (2004). Supporting autonomy in the classroom: Ways teachers encourage student decision making and ownership. *Educational Psychologist, 39*(2), 97–110.

Stiggins, R. (2004). New assessment beliefs for a new school mission. *Phi Delta Kappan, 86*(1), 22–27.

Taylor, L., & Parsons, J. (2011). Improving student engagement. *Current Issues in Education, 14*(1), 1–32.

Texas Accountability Intervention System. (2012). *Critical success factor (CSF) planning guide: Use of quality data to drive instruction.* Accessed at www.taisresources.net/wp-content/uploads/2014/10/Use-of-Quality-Data-to-Drive-Instruction-Planning-Guide.pdf on January 12, 2018.

Vagle, N. (2015). *Design in five: Essential phases to create engaging assessment practice.* Bloomington, IN: Solution Tree Press.

van Barneveld, C. (2008). Using data to improve student achievement. *What Works? Research into Practice, 15.*

Wayman, J. C., Spring, S. D., Lemke, M. A., & Lehr, M. D. (2012). *Using data to inform practice: Effective principal leadership strategies.* Paper presented at the annual meeting of the American Educational Research Association, Vancouver, British Columbia, Canada.

Wiliam, D. (2011). *Embedded formative assessment.* Bloomington, IN: Solution Tree Press.

Zeide, E. (2016). *19 times data analysis empowered students and schools: Which students succeed and why?* Accessed at https://fpf.org/wp-content/uploads/2016/03/Final_19Times-Data_Mar2016–1.pdf on February 2, 2018.

INDEX

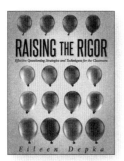

Raising the Rigor: Effective Questioning Strategies and Techniques for the Classroom
Eileen Depka

This user-friendly resource shares questioning strategies and techniques proven to enhance students' critical thinking skills, deepen their engagement, and better prepare them for college and careers. The author also provides a range of templates, surveys, and checklists for planning instruction, deconstructing academic standards, and increasing classroom rigor.

BKF722

Bringing Homework Into Focus: Tools and Tips to Enhance Practices, Design, and Feedback
Eileen Depka

In many classrooms, teachers assign homework out of habit. Learn to design quality homework instead. Prepare students and measure their comprehension by assigning purposeful work, setting clear expectations, and providing feedback as the unit of study unfolds.

BKF616

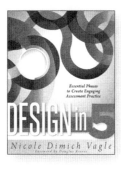

Design in Five: Essential Phases to Create Engaging Assessment Practice
Nicole Dimich Vagle

Discover how to work with your school team to create innovative, effective, engaging assessments using a five-phase design protocol. Explore various types of assessment, learn the traits of quality assessment, and evaluate whether your current assessments meet the design criteria.

BKF604

Got Data? Now What? Creating and Leading Cultures of Inquiry
Laura Lipton and Bruce Wellman

Complete with survey questions for efficient data collection, group work structures, strategies, and tools—along with essential definitions and descriptions of data types—this compelling guide will help you confront data obstacles and turn struggling committees into powerful communities of learners.

BKF530

Solution Tree | Press   a division of
Solution Tree

Visit SolutionTree.com or call 800.733.6786 to order.

"Excellent engagement
in what truly matters
in **assessment**.

Great examples!"

PD Services

Our experts draw from decades of research and their own experiences to bring you
practical strategies for designing and implementing quality assessments. You can choose
from a range of customizable services, from a one-day overview to a multiyear process.

Book your assessment PD today!
888.763.9045

Solution Tree